Soul at Work

Soul at Work

Reflections on a Spirituality of Working

Barbara Smith-Moran

Saint Mary's Press
Christian Brothers Publications
Winona, Minnesota

Note: Pierre Teilhard de Chardin died before inclusive language came into general use. Because changing Teilhard's words would be intrusive in the extreme, his passages have not been altered.

The publishing team for this book included Carl Koch, development editor; Laurie Berg Rohda, manuscript editor; Barbara Bartelson, typesetter; Maurine R. Twait, art director; Tim Foley, illustrator; Kent Linder, cover designer; pre-press, printing, and binding by the graphics division of Saint Mary's Press.

Cover painting: *Barfüsserkirche II (Church of the Minorites II)* (1926), by Lyonel Feininger, oil on canvas, 42¾ by 36⅝ by 2½ inches. Collection Walker Art Center, Minneapolis. Gift of the T. B. Walker Foundation, Gilbert M. Walker Fund, 1943.

The acknowledgments continue on page 109.

Printed in the United States of America

Printing: 9 8 7 6 5 4 3 2 1

Year: 2005 04 03 02 01 00 99 98 97

ISBN 0-88489-396-0

To my husband, Jim,
whose love of Teilhard rubbed off

CONTENTS

FOREWORD

The long-awaited but little-known manuscripts written by Pierre Teilhard de Chardin, SJ, finally saw the light of day after his death in 1955. In the intervening decades, a grateful readership has been stimulated by these writings and by commentaries on Teilhard's insights and his productive life.

Barbara Smith-Moran's book *Soul at Work* is devoted to reflections for those who are prepared to be inspired by Teilhard's spirituality. It is a refreshing, devotional approach, based on the thought and Ignatian spirituality of this Jesuit geologist. Barbara, an Episcopalian priest-scientist, proposes that the reader explore, by prayerful meditation, ways that Teilhard's powerful thought and spirituality may enliven and motivate any person who seeks to find spiritual meaning in and from his or her everyday occupations.

But first a word about Teilhard, the development of his system of thought, and the way he was able to integrate his vigorous pursuit of scientific research with a mysticism that considered these worldly occupations to be sacred work.

Teilhard de Chardin was a fellow Jesuit geologist whom I was privileged to meet on two occasions in the 1950s at meetings of the Geological Society of America. Before Teilhard was ordained a priest in 1912, his study of Henri Bergson's *Evolution Creatrice* helped to stimulate his interest in evolutionary theory and data.

As Teilhard's geological education deepened, his spiritual insights regarding a broader applicability of evolution were drawn from his own familiarity with geological processes generally and from concepts of biological evolution based on paleontological studies specifically. These, in turn, gave rise to new paradigms and insights in his theological and spiritual thought.

Even before the development of the plate tectonics theory, a form of physical evolution of planet Earth, Teilhard came to believe that evolution was a fundamental law of the universe. Believing this to be true in the spiritual realm as well as in the biological realm, Teilhard identified passages in letters of Saint Paul that he interpreted as applicable to an evolution through Christ of the City of God. Teilhard believed that human beings could participate in a meaningful way in the mission of Christ by means of their work in the world.

Teilhard, as a research scientist, was especially interested in a spirituality most appropriate to thinking human beings, a mysticism of knowing. To express these ideas drawn from science, philosophy, and theology, Teilhard had to develop new language, which throughout most of his lifetime was widely mistrusted or misunderstood or both.

Teilhard de Chardin was born in 1881. His service as a stretcher bearer in the trenches in World War I helped to crystallize many of his important concepts. From then until his death in New York on Easter Sunday, 10 April 1955, Teilhard wrote unceasingly. He lived as a young and middle-aged Jesuit in what has been called the anti-Modernist period. This was a time not only of severe censorship, but of stultifying repression of theological, including biblical, scholarship by the Vatican's Holy Office. This resulted in a climate, widespread throughout the church at that time, that was unreceptive to and even repressive of nontraditional ideas, such as Teilhard's, that espoused concepts of evolution. This prompted Teilhard's superiors to welcome the opportunity to assign him to a Jesuit paleontological mission in Peking (now Beijing), China, thus distancing him from the spotlight of controversy in Paris to which his ideas drew him like a magnet.

During the 1920s and 1930s, however, Teilhard continued to develop his thought and his Ignatian spirituality in discussions with fellow Jesuits, other colleagues, and friends in Peking and in the field. His voluminous letters and unpublished manuscripts are now recognized as significant contributions to religious aspects of modern culture.

Upon Teilhard's death in 1955, *The Phenomenon of Man,* with an introduction by the distinguished student of evolution Sir Julian Huxley, was published in French. Next came *The Divine Milieu.* Then volume after volume appeared, with *The Phenomenon of Man* becoming available in English in 1959. The prompt publication of these insightful writings and their sympathetic explication by Teilhard's friend, the highly respected theologian Henri de Lubac, SJ, resulted in many of Teilhard's ideas and the spirit of his ideas being incorporated into the documents of Vatican Council II in the first half of the 1960s.

While a student of theology, Teilhard set out to rethink what is known from Christian revelation about the person of Christ in the context of an evolving universe. He did this because he believed that God, by taking on human nature in the person of Jesus Christ, revealed not only the mystery of God but also the meaning of humankind. Teilhard believed that therein was the key to unlock the ultimate meaning of that evolutionary process that had been set in motion by God and of which the human species is the culmination.

Teilhard, interpreting certain passages of Saint Paul in an evolutionary context, believed that evolution shed new light on the relation of the cosmos to Christ and on the meaning of human activity in building the "noosphere" (named for *nous*, the Greek word for mind), a world-encircling new sphere, not unlike the biosphere, the hydrosphere, and the atmosphere, but which is the product of the activity of human minds and hearts.

Teilhard's system of thought is totally Christocentric because his starting and ending place is Jesus Christ. He interpreted certain passages of Paul to mean that the universe is in the process of evolving toward a completion, or fulfillment, in Jesus as the head of creation.

His unique concept is that all truly human activities of mind and heart, activities of consciousness, contribute to the building of the noosphere. He envisioned that each act of mind and heart, however private or public, contributes incrementally to building the noosphere, thus moving the universe closer to the "Omega Point," or the culmination of evolution. The Omega Point is Teilhard's metaphysical designation for the end point at which Jesus will assume final headship of the universe.

This volume of reflections for meditation was prepared by my friend and colleague the Reverend Barbara Smith-Moran, SOSc, as the result of a need expressed by the leadership of the Episcopal Diocese of Massachusetts for materials to assist scientists and engineers to deepen their spirituality.

I am pleased to say that the Task Force for Cultural Exchange Between Science and Faith, on which I was privileged to serve, decided to experiment with developing a six-week retreat adapted from a twenty-four week Ignatian spirituality retreat that I had been directing at Boston College for several years. Because Teilhard de Chardin was both a devoutly religious person and a scientist, and because we wanted the rather demanding retreat commitment to be carried on while the retreatant was fully involved in everyday activities, we decided to call it "Teilhardian Spirituality in Everyday Life."

These reflections, prepared over the past several years by Pastor Smith-Moran, focus mainly on scriptural passages and on writings of Teilhard de Chardin that shed a new perspective on the world around us and on our role in this evolving universe.

The exercises deal sequentially with six major human issues of importance to those who want to learn to envision their life as counting for something of cosmic value. The exercises offer a Teilhardian perspective that holds that what we do on Sundays by way of worship is part of a piece with the sacred activity of our work during the rest of the week. Teilhard refused to make a distinction between the sacred and the profane because he held that both our worship and the work of our heart and mind help build the earth and the universe. Six perspectives are dealt with in this book under the headings of Vocation or Calling, Preparation, Mission, Success, Setbacks, and Transformation and Transfiguration.

Working together, Pastor Smith-Moran and I have used this book with several group retreats where we asked the dozen retreatants to spend about an hour each day in prayer and other spiritual exercises. They then gathered as a group one night a week to share in a worship service, a meal, and an open exchange of their prayer experiences in the context of their work and other life experiences.

These materials serve as a solid basis for prayerful reflection and contemplation, and the individual stories of life and faith result in a profound bonding of those who have come together as an interdenominational faith community. While there are many resources written for meditative reflection, I believe that this book is unique because of the prayerful Teilhardian perspectives that are incorporated in it. This book's goal is to facilitate contemplation on one's vocation that will inspire action to help build up the City of God and to realize one's individual potential to the full.

James W. Skehan, SJ, SOSc
Associate Professor and Director Emeritus
Weston Observatory
Department of Geology and Geophysics
Boston College

INTRODUCTION

image of a Diego Rivera mural

Lift up your head, Jerusalem, and see the immense multitude of those who build and those who seek; see all those who toil in laboratories, in studios, in factories, in the deserts and in the vast crucible of human society. For all the ferment produced by their labors, in art, in science, in thought, all is for you. (Pierre Teilhard de Chardin, *Hymn of the Universe*, p. 147)

As We Begin

The reflections in this book are intended to encourage a spirituality of everyday work, a feeling for the importance to God of all honest labor and thought. Because God counts on our partnership in building the Reign of God, cocreating the earth, or bringing about the "new Jerusalem," it is right to feel a solid sense of God's call to holy life in worldly occupations: work in science and technology, crafts and trades, agriculture and academe. The truth is, God is intimately involved—more than we know!

Consider the vocabulary of work: job, labor, career, vocation, calling, profession, occupation, employment, trade. The terms *job* and *employment* denote how one spends time to earn money. *Labor* is a more formal term for work (as in Department of Labor), though often it denotes work of the muscular variety. By *profession* we usually mean work with a particular code of conduct and perhaps dress, often requiring certain academic training and formal licensing.

The terms *calling* and *vocation* are, in common usage, reserved almost exclusively for religious work. This convention may have grown out of the belief that God has a deep stake in church-related careers, but somehow cares less for the day-to-day work of the so-called secular sphere. It was commonly thought that those people who involve themselves in secular daily work do so by their own choice, not by vocation. That the church persisted in this mistaken perception was a particular concern of

Pierre Teilhard de Chardin (1881–1955), who was both a Jesuit priest and a research geologist.

For the next six weeks, the reflections in this book invite you to examine your work: how it can be a calling or vocation. From the first week, the reflections use the terms *calling* and *vocation* to denote what many consider their own personal choice of occupations. The application of these terms may provoke some reaction, particularly at first. If you meet with a group to reflect together, the matter of vocabulary may become a topic for shared meditation and discussion.

For some people these reflections may help them see again or for the first time that their work is their true calling. Others may come to the painful conclusion that their present work is not their true calling. Either way, the Spirit will be with you in your reflections to guide, encourage, and inspire you. You need only open your eyes to the transfiguring Light.

Using These Reflections in Solitude

The meditations in this book may be done as a six-week, solitary, homemade retreat. Each week offers a different perspective on the spirituality of vocation. Week 1, Vocation or Calling, asks you to ponder how your work is or can be your vocation. Week 2, Preparation, leads you to consider the steps that have led you to where you are now. Week 3, Mission, should help you to explore your sense of mission, and weeks 4 and 5 invite you to look at your experience of successes and setbacks, respectively. Finally, week 6 calls you to look at the spiritual transformation and transfiguration of your work.

The reflections begin with brief commentaries and passages from Teilhard's writings or from the Bible that focus your attention on God's caring presence in the secular world of work. After this, one or two questions for reflection can help you attend to your own experience. Each reflection ends with a suggestion for conversation with God.

You can spend just a few minutes on each day's reflection or considerably more time. Do the best you can. God blesses a willing soul.

The reflections can be done while riding the subway to work, during the wee hours before your family gets up to meet the day, or during a coffee break when you can shut your office door for a few moments of quiet. Fit them in when and where you can. God is immediately present wherever and whenever you are.

Here are some other suggestions to help you during your homemade retreat:

Open yourself to the power of prayer. Every human experience has a religious dimension. All of life is suffused with God's presence. So remind yourself that God is present as you begin your reflection. Prayer can open your mind and widen your vision. Be open to new ways of seeing God, people, yourself, and your vocation.

Read meditatively. Take your time reading the reflections, savoring the words. If a particular phrase or notion touches you, stay with it. Relish its feeling, meaning, and concerns.

Use the reflections. Each day's meditation offers a couple of ways of reflecting. Some urge you to write your reflections; others suggest that you pray a phrase repeatedly. Pick at least one of the reflections each day—perhaps the one that seems most challenging to your normal way of thinking or praying.

The reflections provide helpful subjects for journal writing. If you write for any length of time, stating honestly what is on your mind and in your heart, you will unearth much about who you are, what deep longings reside in your soul, and how you stand with your work, with others, and with God. If you have never used writing as a means of meditation, try it.

Talk with your God. A simple definition of prayer is the awareness of God and our response to that awareness. One of the responses is to engage the living, gracious God in conversation. So each reflection ends with a suggestion for conversation with God.

Using the Reflections for Group Exploring

Sharing the retreat with a group of kindred spirits can greatly enhance the experience. In fact, the reflections in this book were originally written for group retreats.

In the past, groups of people have decided to meet once each week to share their reflections about the previous week's meditation and prayer and to introduce the subject of the upcoming week's reflections.

The meetings might begin with a short prayer, calling everyone into God's presence. After prayer, the participants might be reminded of the theme of the previous week, using the introduction to that week. Then participants may begin offering their reflections.

End with another time of prayer, during which someone introduces the next week's subject. The appendix includes some passages from the Scriptures and from Teilhard's writings that might be used for each week's ending prayer period.

A Final Thought as You Begin

A story goes like this. Three men were breaking up rocks.

> "What are you doing?" a passerby asks.
> "Making little rocks out of big ones," says the first worker.
> "Earning a living," answers the second.
> "Building a cathedral," says the third.
> (Doris Donnelly, *Spiritual Fitness,* p. 83)

If a passerby saw you working and asked you what you were doing, what would you answer?

Vocation or Calling

Work—sustained effort that has a purpose—may be done for many reasons: to earn money, to fulfill ambitions, to develop a sense of identity, to build the earth, to do what one loves to do, or to answer a call.

Perhaps ideally, a central motivation for our work is that it answers a call from the Spirit of God who dwells within us. Work done from a sense of calling can be described as a vocation, derived from the Latin verb *vocare*—to call. Reflecting on one of the dozens of people interviewed in his book *Working,* Studs Terkel concluded, "I think most of us are looking for a calling, not a job" (p. xxiv). Needless to say, many factors enter into a sense of call: personal talent, interest, need, the guidance of peers, elders, mentors, and role models, and so on.

The sense that a particular calling, vocation, or career fits us sometimes arrives like a flash. More often it slowly dawns on us after a long period of discernment. When it comes like an impulse, the resulting disequilibrium can affect all aspects of our life. We may not know how to begin to talk about it or whom to tell. Family members with a tradition of working in business or music may shake their head in disbelief when a college-aged child announces that she or he has decided to go into biochemistry! Or consider the surprise of a family of nominal or non-churchgoers when one of their own announces that she or he feels called to ministry. Those who have vocational shifts in midlife face another set of questions from family and friends.

On the other hand, if the call takes its time and dawns upon us more gradually, we have an easier time dealing with the slowly shifting equilibrium. The sense that we always somehow knew what we wanted to do may help us plan our life accordingly. The call seems to grow smoothly out of preparations for it.

This week invites you to spend time in prayer and meditation with the story of your own work life. If it is not your practice to think in terms of vocation or calling—you may initially reject such an idea—begin at least to entertain the possibility of such a dynamic between yourself and God. Consider how the work you do is or could become a calling.

A Compelling Vision

Some of us perceive our calling through an experience or image that compels us to say, "Yes, that is what my life should be about." As a young man, Teilhard de Chardin wrote about his own experience of an irresistible vision, "the flash that opened his eyes . . . as a light imprinted deep within."

Even as a young lad, curiosity about stones excited Teilhard. He described it as a passion. This desire called him to geology and supplied him with excitement in his geological research and, as it turned out, in his prayer life, too. In his essay "Awakening to the Cosmos," Teilhard describes his calling:

Already, through the matter that is common to them, all living beings are but one being.

And it is primarily through their all possessing life that they are welded into one.

Life . . . is in some way an extension of matter. With the elements, it retains some of the habits of matter. . . . We should look more closely at the pages of stone on which is written the history of the transformation of living organisms.

For anyone who can turn over those pages patiently, constantly, and religiously, there emerges from them a vast, luminous, picture. . . . The effort to climb upwards is maintained through and beyond partial checks, and the mysterious, unique, life-sap penetrates and makes its way, surrounded though it is by the inconceivable tangle of mechanical and organic activities. Infallibly, it rises up towards some more efficiently knit nervous system, and above all towards brain, where thought will be able to reflect upon itself instantly and unerringly. . . .

First there is the revelation of the unique matter, and then, even more wonderful, that of the unique soul. . . . (Writings in Time of War, pp. 23–25)

The Call

No man who has once experienced this vision can ever forget it. Like the seaman who has known the intoxicating blue of the South Seas—whatever he be whom the ray has touched upon, whether scientist, philosopher, or humble worker—he lives forever with his nostalgia for what is greatest, most durable, for the Absolute whose presence and activity around him he has felt for one moment. The flash that opened his eyes remains as a light imprinted deep within them; and he never ceases to thrill to the awareness of contact with the universe. Others may smile at his vain worries and his odd concern to extend man's consciousness beyond the accepted limits of practical life. But the man with the vision will follow his own road. . . . Deeper than the soul of individuals, vaster than the human group, there is a vital fluid or spirit of things, there is some absolute, that draws us and yet lies hidden. If we are to see its features, to answer its call and understand its meaning, and if we are to learn to live more, we must *plunge boldly* into the vast current of things and see whither its flow is carrying us. (*Writings in Time of War*, pp. 27–28)

If you have the urge to critique Teilhard's metaphysical, cosmic vision, try to resist doing so at this point, reflecting instead on the memories of life calling to you or other reactions that this passage stirs up. Reflect upon your own version of what drives or unites the cosmos.

- What is the vision that guides your life and work?
- No matter what your current profession, what is your mission in life? In a sentence, try to describe the core guiding principle of your life, your calling. ⎯ to deliver, write & inform

Converse with God about your sense of calling or, if your calling seems vague or even absent, ask for some understanding and patience.

Peace & the Part

DAY 2

A Call *From* and *To*

> [God] said to Abram, "Go from your country and your kindred and your father's house to the land that I will show you." (Genesis 12:1)

> [God commanded Moses:] "Go and assemble the elders of Israel, and say to them, . . . 'I declare that I will bring you up out of the misery of Egypt, to the land of the Canaanites, . . . a land flowing with milk and honey.'" (Exodus 3:16–17)

> [Jesus] saw a tax collector named Levi, sitting at the tax booth; and he said to him, "Follow me." (Luke 5:27)

Abram, Moses, and Levi each received a call away *from* an old life and *to* something new, unseen, and unfamiliar, but something that God had in mind for them. Calls from the Holy One are usually like this: they draw us from something, but to something better—although this may not be immediately evident.

- In light of your experience of making transitions and taking risks in life and in work, imagine what Abram, Moses, and Levi might have felt.
- Ponder the aspects of the life you left behind in order to risk journeying to a "new place," metaphorically speaking.
- Did you leave behind a land of affliction or a land of affection? a place of comfort, a rat race, a trap—or something else?
- What "milk and honey" did the new place offer: opportunities? new challenges? new friends? new questions? a new sense of who you are and what your true calling is?

Converse with the Spirit of Wisdom about any fears, regrets, gratitude, and questions that you have about your calling *from* and your calling *to*.

Jesus Calls Disciples

The stories of the call to discipleship are among our most cherished Gospel stories. Mark's account of the call of the fishermen Simon and Andrew contains that wonderful play on words, "'Follow me and I will make you fish for people'" (1:17).

John's Gospel tells the detailed, richly symbolic story of Jesus' calling the Samaritan woman to discipleship. She may or may not have actually traveled with Jesus, Simon, Andrew, Mary Magdalene, and the other named disciples. The Gospel account does not say one way or the other. We do know that she followed Jesus with her heart, and this is far more important.

Read the familiar story again. This time use your imagination to enter the story yourself.

> [Jesus] came to a Samaritan city called Sychar, near the plot of ground that Jacob had given to his son Joseph. Jacob's well was there, and Jesus, tired out by his journey, was sitting by the well. It was about noon.
>
> A Samaritan woman came to draw water, and Jesus said to her, "Give me a drink." . . . The Samaritan woman said to him, "How is it that you, a Jew, ask a drink of me, a woman of Samaria?" . . . Jesus answered her, "If you knew the gift of God, and who it is that is saying to you, 'Give me a drink,' you would have asked him, and he would have given you living water." The woman said to him, "Sir, you have no bucket, and the well is deep. Where do you get that living water? Are you greater than our ancestor Jacob, who gave us the well, and with his sons and his flocks drank from it?" Jesus said to her, "Everyone who drinks of this water will be thirsty again, but those who drink of the water that I will give them will never be thirsty. The water that I will give will become in them a spring of water gushing up to eternal life." The woman said to him, "Sir, give me this water, so that I may never be thirsty or have to keep coming here to draw water."

Jesus said to her, "Go, call your husband, and come back." The woman answered him, "I have no husband." Jesus said to her, "You are right in saying, 'I have no husband'; for you have had five husbands, and the one you have now is not your husband. What you have said is true!" The woman said to him, "Sir, I see that you are a prophet. Our ancestors worshiped on this mountain; but you say that the place where people must worship is in Jerusalem." Jesus said to her, "Woman, believe me, the hour is coming when you will worship [God] neither on this mountain nor in Jerusalem. You worship what you do not know; we worship what we know, for salvation is from the Jews. But the hour is coming, and is now here, when the true worshipers will worship [God] in spirit and truth. . . . God is spirit, and those who worship [God] must worship in spirit and truth." The woman said to him, "I know that Messiah is coming" (who is called Christ). "When he comes, he will proclaim all things to us." Jesus said to her, "I am he, the one who is speaking to you."

. . . Then the woman left her water jar, and went back into the city. She said to the people, "Come and see a man who told me everything I have ever done! He cannot be the Messiah, can he?" They left the city and were on their way to him.

Many Samaritans from that city believed in him because of the woman's testimony. (John 4:5–30,39)

Close your eyes and set the scene, picturing the town and the well. Let your imagination decide what the weather is. Feel it, and breathe in the air. See Jesus there, needing help, refreshment, and rest. See the woman, and hear the two of them talk and react to one another. The woman's name has not been preserved, but perhaps, at some level, you recognize her and know her name. If not, give her a name you think is right. As the scene plays in your imagination, you may feel that you want to approach Jacob's well yourself.

- What draws you closer? Or what keeps you at a distance?
- Perhaps the woman will call you to come and see this man: "He cannot be the Messiah, can he?"

Converse with Jesus about what you believe he is calling you to do and to be.

The Choice to Say No

Many quite legitimate reasons may tempt us to resist answering a call in the affirmative. Pressing matters may demand immediate attention ("Lord, first let me go and bury my father" [Matthew 8:21]). Or an answer needs to be postponed until after further deliberation. A search of psyche and soul may be necessary to test the legitimacy of a felt call.

Advisers we trust and respect may counsel us not to take the road that pulls at our heart and mind. In Teilhard's experience, the church discouraged a vocation to science as somehow tainted or second-rate. From the battlefront in France in 1916, he wrote:

> The Church, then, must do more than tolerate [progress in science], and accept it, as an inevitable compulsion or a necessary stimulus. She must, as we anxiously wait for her to do, recognize it officially; she must adopt it in its principle (if not in all its methods); she must unreservedly encourage bold experiments and attempts made to open new roads. So long as she neglects to include, among the Christian's essential obligations, *the sacred duty of research,* in other words his being bound, under pain of sin, to assist in the specific and temporal betterment of the earth—it will be a waste of time for her apologists to put forward the illustrious names of scientists who have also been men of prayer. She will still have to prove that if science flourishes in her wake, too, it is *by right* that this is so, and *under her influence* and not in spite of her or through a happy chance. . . .
>
> For these [Christians called to science], *not to seek,* not to plumb to its depths the domain of energies and of thought, not to strive to exhaust the Real, will be a grievous *triple fault,* a fault of *infidelity,* . . . *a fault of presumption,* . . . *a fault,* thirdly, *of intellectual intransigence.* . . .

Nihil intentatum—nothing left untried—is their motto (the very motto, indeed, of evolution), which, in the fulfillment of nature's lofty destiny, *brings them into line with the noblest spirit of Revelation.* (*Writings in Time of War*, pp. 88–89)

Abram, Moses, Levi, Mary, Mary Magdalene, the Samaritan woman, Simon, Andrew, and Teilhard were free to say no to the call they each received to do what they knew in their heart was God's highest hope for them.

- What, if anything, has blocked or discouraged you in your pursuit of vocation? Is anything blocking the way even now?
- Do the discouragements and roadblocks have a positive side at all? Is there a value to resistance?
- Do you recall any important times when your answer was no?
- Ponder your most important yes to your calling.

In some manner, celebrate with the Creator the yeses you have made to your calling.

DAY 5

Who Calls?

Like us, our biblical ancestors needed to know the identity of the One calling before they would respond. Recall these examples:

> Moses replied to God, "What should I say if the people of Israel ask me, 'What is the name of the one who spoke to you?' What name should I give them?" (Adapted from Exodus 3:13)

> A man wrestled with [Jacob] until daybreak. . . . Then Jacob asked him, "Please, tell me your name." (Genesis 32:24–29)

> God called again, "Samuel!" Samuel got up and went to Eli, and said, "Here I am, for you called me." But he said, "I did not call, my son; lie down again." (1 Samuel 3:6)

> [Saul] fell to the ground and heard a voice saying to him, "Saul, Saul, why do you persecute me?" He asked, "Who are you, Lord?" (Acts 9:4–5)

How can we follow a call until we are certain of the character of the one who is calling? Determining the identity of the caller is certainly prudent.

The God of Abraham and Sarah, Isaac and Rebekah, Jacob, Leah, and Rachel carries credentials that inspire our confidence and devotion, credentials based on love and faithfulness in relationship with our spiritual fathers and mothers. We feel pulled to follow the call of such a God, if we find in our prayers that God is indeed the one calling. Teilhard said:

> Lord, it is you, who, through the imperceptible goadings of sense-beauty, penetrated my heart in order to make its life flow out into yourself. You came down into me by means of a tiny scrap of created reality; and then, suddenly, you unfurled your immensity before my eyes and displayed yourself to me as Universal Being.

So the basic mystical intuition issues in the discovery of a supra-real unity diffused throughout the immensity of the world.

In that *milieu,* at once divine and cosmic, in which he had at first observed only a simplification and as it were a spiritualization of space, the seer, faithful to the light given him, now perceives the gradual delineation of the form and attributes of an ultimate *element* in which all things find their definitive consistency.

And then he begins to measure more exactly the joys, and the pressing demands, of that mysterious presence to which he has surrendered himself. (*Hymn of the Universe,* p. 91)

Vocational decisions usually involve many considerations other than God's hopes and plans, which may not get even a first thought! Fortunately, our inattention does not deter God who can and does manage to get things done through all sorts of human motivation.

Trying to separate God's call from personal choice is sometimes about as counterproductive as rooting up the weeds before the wheat field has ripened. In the following passage, we get an indication of how Teilhard worked out his own solution to the wheat and weeds problem:

God is not to be found indiscriminately in the things that thwart us in life or the trials we have to suffer—but solely *at the point of balance* between our desperate efforts to grow greater and the resistance to our domination that we meet from outside. . . .

It was a joy to me, O God, in the midst of the struggle, to feel that in developing myself I was increasing the hold that you had upon me; it was a joy to me, too, under the inner thrust of life or amid the favourable play of events, to abandon myself to your Providence. Now that I have found the joy of utilizing all forms of growth to make you, or to let you, grow in me. (*Let Me Explain,* p. 127)

Teilhard experienced God's presence in all life's events, in the fullness of creation. He discerned who was calling him, according to whether the urge led toward growth, integration, and fullness, or toward destruction, disunity, and despair. The names of the God of Abraham and Sarah, Mary, Paul, and Teilhard are Love, One, Hope, Faithfulness.

- Reflect upon the identity of the one calling you in the past and in the present.
- If you are not certain who is calling you, then ask for some identification and credentials. Use Teilhard's criteria.

Open your soul to the One calling you about your relationship with your spiritual fathers and mothers right now.

DAY 6

Surprises

Our tradition and experience teach us that God is often a God of surprises. The Bible offers many stories about people being surprised by God's calling. Here are just two examples:

> [God] appeared to Abraham by the oaks of Mamre, as he sat at the entrance of his tent in the heat of the day. He looked up and saw three men standing near him (18:1–2). One said, "I will surely return to you in due season, and your wife Sarah shall have a son." And Sarah was listening at the tent entrance behind him. Now Abraham and Sarah were old, advanced in age; it had ceased to be with Sarah after the manner of women. So Sarah laughed to herself (18:10–12). [God] did for Sarah as . . . promised. Sarah conceived, and bore Abraham a son in his old age. (Genesis 21:1–2)

> The whole congregation of the Israelites complained against Moses and Aaron in the wilderness. The Israelites said to them, "If only we had died by the hand of [God] in the land of Egypt . . . for you have brought us out into this wilderness to kill this whole assembly with hunger" (2–3). In the evening quails came up and covered the camp; and in the morning . . . when the layer of dew lifted, there on the surface of the wilderness was a fine flaky substance, as fine as frost on the ground (13–14). The house of Israel called it manna . . . and the taste of it was like wafers made with honey. (Exodus 16:31)

God is "familiar with all my ways" (Psalm 139:3). "[God] created my inmost being and knit me together in my mother's womb" (Psalm 139:13). So perhaps the surprise in a call comes not so much because God surprises us, but because, with God's grace, we suddenly see into our inmost being for the first time and see the call knit deeply into our soul. Fortunately, surprising calls that we attribute to God offer us challenges, enlightenment, and food for the soul—when seen with the eyes of faith.

- Do these stories remind you of any surprises you have experienced along the way, as you have followed your vocation?
- Were any of them delightful, easy reminders of God's presence and providence?
- What about the painful surprises?

Converse with the Creator about any other surprising calls that might yet be discovered, or about calls you may have tried *not* to discover.

WEEK 2

Preparation

Hopefully, week 1 helped you gain a clearer perspective on and a keener appreciation of your calling. This week's endeavor is to review the preparation for your calling, all the steps that have led you to be where you are now.

Preparation for a chosen vocation often begins purposefully, like graduate students researching a topic or American Indians seeking a vision. Retrospection often reveals, however, that many events before a particular time of decision seem to have been leading up to that point, as if in unconscious preparation. For example, many people in caregiving professions (medicine, nursing, ministry, psychology, social work) discover, often to their surprise, that the experience of loss, abuse, or serious illness in their own childhood has actually served to prepare them to accept a vocation of service to others in pain. Seen through the eyes of the four Gospel writers, everything Jesus did and said had within it some element of preparation for his death, Resurrection, and glorification.

This week's exercises can stimulate you to recall the choices you consciously made in preparing for your vocation(s) and also to reflect upon how certain events in your life have served to prepare you for challenges you have had to face.

DAY 1

Jesus Prepares for His Ministry

A good deal of every person's life, no matter how active, is carried out in private. Until he was about thirty years old, Jesus led such a "hidden life."

Read meditatively the following Scripture story that describes in symbolic and dramatic terms Jesus' change in vocation. Ponder any parallels between his preparation for a change in direction and the course of your own vocation.

In those days John the Baptist appeared in the wilderness of Judea, proclaiming, "Repent, for the kingdom of heaven has come near." This is the one of whom the prophet Isaiah spoke when he said,

"The voice of one crying out in the wilderness:
'Prepare the way of the Lord,
    make [the] paths straight.'"

. . . Then Jesus came from Galilee to John at the Jordan, to be baptized by him. . . . And when Jesus had been baptized, just as he came up from the water, suddenly the heavens were opened to him and he saw the Spirit of God descending like a dove and alighting on him. And a voice from heaven said, "This is my Son, the Beloved, with whom I am well pleased."

Then Jesus was led up by the Spirit into the wilderness to be tempted by the devil. He fasted forty days and forty nights, and afterwards he was famished. The tempter came and said to him, "If you are the Son of God, command these stones to become loaves of bread." But he answered, "It is written,

'One does not live by bread alone,
    but by every word that comes from the mouth of God.'"

Then the devil took him to the holy city and placed him on the pinnacle of the temple, saying to him, "If you are the Son of God, throw yourself down; for it is written,

'[God] will command [the] angels concerning you,'
and 'On their hands they will bear you up,
so that you will not dash your foot against a stone.'"
Jesus said, "Again it is written, 'Do not put . . . your God to the test.'"

Again, the devil took him to a very high mountain and showed him all the kingdoms of the world and their splendor, and [the devil] said to him, "All these I will give you, if you will fall down and worship me." Jesus said . . . , "Away with you, Satan! for it is written,
'Worship . . . your God,
and serve only [God].'"
Then the devil left him, and suddenly angels came and waited on him.

Now when Jesus heard that John had been arrested, he withdrew to Galilee. He left Nazareth and made his home in Capernaum by the sea. . . .

From that time Jesus began to proclaim, "Repent, for the kingdom of heaven has come near." (Matthew 3:1–17; 4:1–17)

Before his baptism at the river, Jesus probably learned many useful skills. From the story of his appearance in the Temple, we know that he had been instructed in the Scriptures and must have learned to pray. In this story from Matthew, chapters 3 and 4, Jesus' preparation took definitive steps: baptism and the recognition by the Spirit, fasting, prayer, overcoming the temptations to abandon his ministry, and the first public proclamations.

Like Jesus, we too go through steps in preparing for and assenting to our call.

- Reflect upon what may have motivated Jesus to live and work so long as a carpenter (as tradition has it) before entering his "second career." How did he spend his days? his years? How did this prepare him for his public life?
- Recall the decisions you had to make in pursuit of a vocation. Were your decisions accompanied by doubts, fears, and temptations? Ponder those decisions. Then recognize your own strengths and interests in moving toward your call.

Ask for the grace you need to embrace fully or to stay the course of your vocation. Like Jesus, you may have been tempted to abandon what you know to be your true call.

(This reflection is an adaptation from James W. Skehan, SJ, *Place Me with Your Son: Ignatian Spirituality in Everyday Life.*)

DAY 2

Preparing the Soil

The harvest does not begin with sowing of the seeds. First, the land must be prepared, opened, cultivated, and fertilized. In this sense, the gardener prepares to prepare for the harvest.

In seeking our own role in cocreating with God, considering how we prepare can help us understand and respond to the call when it comes. We actually have a call to preparation for our vocation. The parable of the talents can be interpreted in this context. The servant best suited for the steward's vocation is the one who applies some effort and ingenuity when put to the test during the householder's absence: in preparation for the homecoming, the servant with a strong sense of vocation multiplies the original talent left in his or her stewardship.

Teilhard de Chardin clearly recognized that a vocation is accompanied by the call to always be growing and developing:

First, develop yourself, Christianity says to the Christian.

Books about the spiritual life do not as a general rule throw this first phase of Christian perfection into relief. Perhaps it seems too obvious to deserve mention, or seems to belong too completely to the "natural" sphere, or possibly it is too dangerous to be insisted upon—whatever the reason, these books usually remain silent on the subject or take it for granted. This is a fault and an omission. Although the majority of people understand it easily enough, and although its essentials are common to the ethics of both layman and religious, the duty of human perfection, like the whole universe, has been renewed, recast, supernaturalised, in the kingdom of God. It is a truly Christian duty to grow . . . and to make one's talents bear fruit, even though they be natural. It is part of the essentially Catholic vision to look upon the world as maturing—not only in each individual or in each nation, but in the whole human race—a specific power of knowing and loving whose transfigured term is charity, but whose roots and elemental sap lie in the discovery and [the love] of everything that is true and beautiful in creation. . . . The effort of mankind, even in realms inaccurately called profane, must, in the Christian life, assume the role of a holy and unifying operation. It is the collaboration, trembling with love, which we give to the hands of God, concerned to attire and prepare us (and the world) for the final union through sacrifice. Understood in this way, the care which we devote to personal achievement and embellishment is no more than a gift begun. (*The Divine Milieu*, pp. 70–71)

"It is a truly Christian duty to grow . . . and to make one's talents bear fruit." God's grace steadily invites us to grow. And so the Creator invites us to embrace creation and discover its lessons, to open our souls in charity to people, and to learn from and unite ourselves to them. Living this way becomes part of our preparation to our unique vocation and "a gift begun."

- Reread Teilhard's words slowly, meditatively. When a phrase strikes you as especially challenging, confirming, or inspiring, stay with it until its particular import becomes clearer to you.
- Teilhard was a research geologist, but he meditated on Scripture, discussed matters of the soul with friends, and pondered the wonders of creation. Reflect on your own preparation for vocation. Besides training for a specific call, how are you preparing your soul for growth?

Converse with the Creator about the status of your own preparations for growth of all kinds.

DAY 3

Silent Readiness for Revelation

Divine revelations come from many sources: the Bible, nature, the love between two people. The Chinese sage Lao-tzu declared that "silence is the great revelation." Many of us probably have some comprehension of this truth, but so much noise clutters our day and demands our attention that silence seems impossible to attain. Besides all the external noise, internal clatter can create a din in our mind.

If we are going to learn the lessons of nature, we must pay attention to nature. If silence is going to reveal anything to us, we need to be silent.

Take a comfortable posture and close your eyes. For two minutes or so, try to attain silence, as total a silence of heart and mind as possible.

If your mind darts from topic to topic or scene to scene, do not worry. Even our distractions can teach us what is really on our mind and in our heart. So pay attention to them.

Sitting quietly again, close your eyes and attend to the meanderings of your mind. Observe each thought and feeling, and then let it go. Another will follow.

Now listen to the silence that permits you to attend to your mind's wanderings.

No matter how short the time is that you attain silence, this silence is a start. Being quiet and mindful invites the silence to grow. Out of the silence, revelations about our self, about the Holy One, and about creation come. As the late Anthony de Mello claimed, "Silence will reveal yourself to you. That is its first revelation: your *self*. And in and through this revelation you will attain things that money cannot buy, things like wisdom and serenity and joy and God" (*Sadhana*, p. 10).

Silence requires effort, patience, and attention.

- While sitting alertly with your eyes closed, be silent for five minutes or so. When you open your eyes, write down or note whatever you observed—no matter how seemingly trivial—while your mind wandered or in the intervals of silence. Keep in mind De Mello's words:

> The important thing is that you have become aware. . . . The content of your awareness is less important than the quality of the awareness. As the quality improves, your silence will deepen. And as your silence deepens, you will experience change. And you will discover, to your delight, that revelation is not knowledge. Revelation is power; a mysterious power that brings transformation. (*Sadhana*, p. 11)

- Ponder this: How can I build periods of silence into my day—even just moments of silence—as part of my preparation for my calling?

Rest in silence in the Divine Presence. If thoughts and feelings flood in, just offer them up and let go of them.

DAY 4

Waiting and Hoping

Preparing for understanding, light, or revelations often demands hopeful waiting from us. Many of us are not very practiced at either waiting or hoping. This is an opportunity to ponder both spiritual disciplines.

Spend five minutes in silence in preparation for revelation. Then read the following story. As you read, place yourself in the scene. Let your imagination notice the weather, the texture of the ground, and the smell of the place. Notice your own position there: Are you a stranger to this place or a frequenter?

> At the time of a Jewish festival, Jesus journeyed to Jerusalem.
>
> By the Sheep Gate in Jerusalem, there is a pool named in Hebrew Beth-zatha. It has five porticoes. Many blind, lame, and paralyzed people lay in these colonnades. One person there had been ill for thirty-eight years. Jesus realized immediately that this person had been laying near the pool for a long time and asked, "Do you seek healing?"
>
> "Sir," the poor person answered, "I don't have anyone with me who can lower me into the pool when the water is stirred up. While I am getting there on my own, someone else gets in ahead of me."
>
> Jesus replied, "Stand. Fold up your mat. Walk."
>
> Immediately, the person was healed. (Adapted from John 5:1–9)

Imagine waiting thirty-eight years to be healed. This is the hopeful waiting that is sometimes required of us while preparing for our calling. Meditate on the story further.

- Let your imagination ponder these questions:
  - □ What sort of people sit by the pool?
  - □ What are they doing while they wait?
  - □ What about the passersby?
  - □ Does Jesus come by out of curiosity, or does he come with intentions?

38

- □ What do you think of the person Jesus speaks with?
- □ Do you know him or her?
- □ Thirty-eight years is a veritable lifetime. What has this person been doing all that time?
- □ How has the illness affected his or her life?
- □ What about Jesus' question, "Do you seek healing?" Why does the person answer the way he or she does? If you were in the same position, how would you answer?
- Would you like to approach Jesus and speak with him, or ask him to come over to where you are? Why or why not? Do you need any healing yourself? Would you like to ask questions of him? What would you like him to tell you? What would you like him to do with or for you? What difference would it make?

Converse with Jesus about waiting and hoping for healing and about being called to "stand, fold up your mat, walk."

DAY 5

Connecting to God's Larger Purpose

On the night of his arrest, Jesus experienced the most intense anguish. His conflict with the religious and political authorities had reached a crisis point. The scene in the Garden of Gethsemane only begins to suggest his torment:

> They went to a place called Gethsemane; and [Jesus] said to his disciples, "Sit here while I pray." He took with him Peter and James and John, and began to be distressed and agitated. And he said to them, "I am deeply grieved, even to death; remain here, and keep awake." And going a little farther, he threw himself on the ground and prayed that, if it were possible, the hour might pass from him. He said, "Abba, Father, for you all things are possible; remove this cup from me; yet, not what I want, but what you want." (Mark 14:32–36)

There is no evidence that Jesus considered turning back from his mission, but seeing its consequences caused him this agony. After all, good decisions can come to naught or can culminate in difficult junctures. Then, too, sometimes we kick ourselves for what we identify in retrospect as a mistake or a bad decision during our journey.

One preparation we can make for the hard times, the fearful times, is to develop a sense of cooperating with some larger purpose or plan of God's, of participating in some ultimate good. Then we can find the courage to make hard decisions with wisdom and integrity.

Teilhard had a profound understanding of his own role in God's ongoing creative process, even—and perhaps especially—in difficult times. In *Hymn of the Universe,* he wrote:

> The aspect of life which most stirs my soul is the ability to share in an undertaking, in a reality, more enduring than myself: it is in this spirit and with this purpose in view that I try to perfect myself and to master things a little more. When death lays its hand upon me it will leave intact these

things, these ideas, these realities which are more solid and more precious than I. . . .

In the lowliness of fear and the thrill of danger we carry on the work of completing an element which the mystical body of Christ can draw *only* from us. Thus to our peace is added the exaltation of creating, perilously, an eternal work which will not exist without us. (Pp. 115–116)

The fifteenth-century English mystic Julian of Norwich wrote of a similar sense of hope derived from her mission. The following passage from *Revelations of Divine Love* demonstrates the depth of her hope:

At one time our good Lord said, "All shall be well," and at another time he said, "You yourself shall see that all manner of things shall be well." In these two sayings the soul took several different understandings.

One was that he wills that we grasp that he pays attention not only to noble and great things but also to little and small, lowly and simple things. He takes heed of both the one and the other, which is what he means when he says, "All manner of things shall be well." He wills that we understand that not even the smallest thing will be forgotten.

Another understanding of these two sayings is this: As we see it, there are many deeds evilly done. So great is the harm they cause, that it seems to us impossible that they could ever come to good. We look upon these deeds sorrowing and mourning so that, on their account, we cannot be at rest in the blissful contemplation of God as we should be. The cause is this: the reasoning we can use now is so blind, so low and so simple that we cannot know the lofty, marvelous wisdom, the power and the goodness, of the blessed Trinity. That is what he means where he says, "You yourself shall see that all manner of things shall be well." It is as if he said, "Pay attention now, faithfully and trustfully, and at the last end you shall see it in truth, in the fulness of joy." (P. 131)

At the difficult junctures, trust in God's mercy and retain a sense that we participate in the work of God, drawing us on and keeping us from despair. A scientist would never expect to make a startling breakthrough without years of study, research, and thought. How can we be prepared for the grace of spiritual transformation in difficult times without prayerful preparation?

41

- What "undertaking" or sense of "completing an element" within the mystical body of Christ gives you purpose or mission?
- Have you done sufficient prayerful preparation so that when the hard times confront you, you can say with Julian, "All shall be well"?

Turn to the Living God. Converse about the difficult junctures you have come upon and that you suspect await you down the road. Ask for the faith to know that all will be well.

DAY 6

Preparing to Hear God's Word

So far this week you have considered preparing for your vocation through practicing silence, learning to trust, developing a sense of mission, and so on. Hearing God's word, so key in recognizing our vocation, also requires preparing. Jesus' parable of the sower deals with the value of preparation to receive God's word. Here is Luke's version:

> "A sower went out to sow . . . seed; . . . some fell on the path and was trampled on, and the birds of the air ate it up. Some fell on the rock; and as it grew up, it withered for lack of moisture. Some fell among thorns, and the thorns grew with it and choked it. Some fell into good soil, and when it grew, it produced a hundredfold." . . .
>
> Then [Jesus'] disciples asked what this parable meant. He said, . . . "Now the parable is this: The seed is the word of God. The ones on the path are those who have heard; then the devil comes and takes away the word from their hearts, so that they may not believe and be saved. The ones on the rock are those who, when they hear the word, receive it with joy. But these have no root; they believe only for a while and in a time of testing fall away. As for what fell among the thorns, these are the ones who hear; but as they go on their way, they are choked by the cares and riches and pleasures of life, and their fruit does not mature. But as for that in the good soil, these are the ones who, when they hear the word, hold it fast in an honest and good heart, and bear fruit with patient endurance." (8:5–15)

The author of this Gospel goes on, in the Book of Acts, to give us a good example of "soil" properly prepared: he was a Gentile, surprisingly, and an official of the Ethiopian court. Though not a Jew, he worshiped God according to the Jewish understanding. He studied the Hebrew Scriptures, thus preparing himself to meet up with the likes of Philip, who helped God's word germinate properly:

43

There was an Ethiopian eunuch, a court official of the Candace, queen of the Ethiopians, in charge of her entire treasury. He had come to Jerusalem to worship and was returning home; seated in his chariot, he was reading the prophet Isaiah. Then the Spirit said to Philip, "Go over to this chariot and join it." So Philip ran up to it and heard him reading the prophet Isaiah. He asked, "Do you understand what you are reading?" He replied, "How can I, unless someone guides me?" And he invited Philip to get in and sit beside him. Now the passage of the scripture that he was reading was this:

"Like a sheep he was led to the slaughter,
    and like a lamb silent before its shearer,
        so he does not open his mouth.
In his humiliation justice was denied him.
    Who can describe his generation?
        For his life is taken away from the earth."

The eunuch asked Philip, "About whom, may I ask you, does the prophet say this, about himself or about someone else?" Then Philip began to speak, and starting with this scripture, he proclaimed to him the good news about Jesus. As they were going along the road, they came to some water; and the eunuch said, "Look, here is water! What is to prevent me from being baptized?" He commanded the chariot to stop, and both of them, Philip and the eunuch, went down into the water, and Philip baptized him. (Acts 8:27–38)

Philip compellingly reinterpreted the Hebrew prophetic Scriptures for the treasurer, according to the new understanding of them taught by the followers of Jesus. Similarly, after Paul met the Risen Christ on the road to Damascus, he spent an important period of time in study and instruction, which completed his Christian conversion. These periods of directed study of the Scriptures might be considered the first examples of Christian spiritual direction. Consider the time you spend with these meditations on your vocation to be a preparation for something more. Meditate upon these Scripture stories, relating them to your own story.

- What role do the Scriptures have in opening your heart to your vocation as a follower of Christ? Do you ponder the Scriptures, study them, and let them touch your soul and inform your life?

- Do you have some sense yet of what you are preparing for, even at this moment?

Recall that Christ travels with you throughout your journey— even right now. Ask for his word to enflame your soul with a sense of your call.

WEEK 3

Mission

Finding our mission may have a great deal of serendipity about it, but it usually includes a sense of call. Acting upon the conviction—maybe suspicion or hope is more accurate—that we may be called or well suited to a particular vocation, we enter a period of schooling with a mentor or guide. Ready or not, we are sent out to do the work for which we have been trained. The time for individuation, the beginning of our unique mission, begins here. For some of us, that time seems to come too soon, before we feel ready or confident. Others may feel that it has been forever in coming.

Sometimes preparation and mission become a cycle, repeated several times, as a career develops and changes over a lifetime. In the communal life of faith, a weekly rhythmic cycle is established between the calling in and the sending forth: the call to worshipful study, nourishment, and fellowship on the Sabbath, concluding with a dismissal to do God's work in the world. In professional academic life, the seven-year sabbatical cycle encourages vocational refreshment and renewal. Many types of work require or encourage ongoing education and periodic recertification.

This week's exercises invite you to reflect upon your own mission as a worker in the world and as a Christian. No matter what your profession—scientist, teacher, accountant, manager, artist, or chef—recall your mentors and the attitudes encouraged by them. Try to identify the cycles of mission in your own life.

DAY 1

The Mission of the Seventy and Us

The mission of Jesus' followers is the same as that of the one whom they follow. As he began his public life, Jesus declared that his mission was "'to bring good news to the poor, . . . to proclaim release to the captives and recovery of sight to the blind, to let the oppressed go free, to proclaim the year of [God's] favor'" (Luke 4:18–19). Later, Jesus repeated his call to mission:

> The Lord appointed seventy others and sent them on ahead of him in pairs to every town and place where he himself intended to go. He said to them, "The harvest is plentiful, but the laborers are few; therefore ask the Lord of [the] harvest to send out laborers into the harvest. Go on your way. See, I am sending you out like lambs into the midst of wolves. Carry no purse, no bag, no sandals; and greet no one on the road. Whatever house you enter, first say, 'Peace to this house!' And if anyone is there who shares in peace, your peace will rest on that person; but if not, it will return to you. Remain in the same house, eating and drinking what they provide, for the laborer deserves to be paid. Do not move about from house to house. Whenever you enter a town and its people welcome you, eat whatever is set before you; cure the sick who are there, and say to them, 'The kingdom of God has come near to you.' But whenever you enter a town and they do not welcome you, go out into its streets and say, 'Even the dust of your town that clings to our feet, we wipe off in protest against you. Yet know this: the kingdom of God has come near.' . . .
>
> "Whoever listens to you listens to me, and whoever rejects you rejects me, and whoever rejects me rejects the one who sent me." (Luke 10:1–16)

When reading this passage, we might be tempted to say, "He's not talking to me." True, the specifics of Jesus' call to mission may not apply, but the general terms of his words are directed at all those who call themselves Christian: do good, heal where you

48

can, liberate oppressed people, live simply, and speak the Good News that God loves us.

- Read the story from Luke again. Use your imagination to bring it alive, placing yourself among the seventy people commissioned by Jesus. What specific "field" does he want you to sow and harvest in? Do you feel prepared to go? What things make you nervous? Who is your companion, or who are your colleagues in mission?

- Try to extend the story imaginatively beyond the limits of the Gospel account. What places do you visit with your companion, and what is your reception there? Do any "wolves" present themselves for you to deal with?

Ask God for the wisdom and courage you need to start out on your mission, and pray for your companions on the journey.

Day 2

Soul Healing for Mission

We have a mission outward and a mission inward. Just as Jesus healed people and spread the Good News, he also withdrew from time to time to be alone and pray, to let God heal his soul. In Jesus' name, we are called to heal our soul, too. Teilhard wrote:

> By his fidelity [a man] must *construct*—starting with the most natural zone of his own self—a work, an *opus*, into which something enters from all the elements of the earth. *He makes his own soul* throughout all his earthly days. (*The Divine Milieu*, p. 29)

Soul making! A wonderful image of our inner mission! Such a mission certainly involves inner healing. Sometimes we need the aid of professionals; sometimes we do not. Whatever healing needs to be done, God's grace goes with us to give us health for the journey.

■ This exercise invites us to revisit and rework memories of past injustices as part of our ongoing mission of inner healing. This meditation is adapted from an exercise in Anthony de Mello's book, *Sadhana*, pages 67–69.

We can drag along with us injuries and half-healed scars from long ago that still affect us in ways that we may be unconscious of. At one point we may have been consumed by grief over a lost love or the death of a friend or parent. As time passed, the pain may have drifted down into our unconscious. Unless we were able to integrate the experience into our life, it might still affect us by making us suspicious of people or afraid to get close to anyone.

A spouse may hold a profound grudge from an old hurt. Over time the grudge festers unrecognized and only shows itself through sarcasm or sudden chilling toward the other. Love may still burn, but the old grudge dampens the flames periodically and can, over time, put the fire out completely.

Some of us labor under ancient guilt feelings that obscure our vision of the goodness and Good News all around us.

Periodic revisiting of past hurts can help us to heal them before they become obstacles to our outer mission.

Stretch your body. Then sit alertly but comfortably. Breathe deeply and slowly for a while, inviting God's spirit into your soul and life-giving air into your body.

Revisit a story from your past of wounding, grieving, or being afraid, angry, or desperate. As in a movie, set the scene: Who was there, what happened, and what effects did it have then?

Now, ask God: How were you present during this time? How were you trying to help me?

Invite Christ into the event. Ask him for the help you need to get past the pain. Talk to him about all your feelings and desires connected to the event. Attend to what he says.

If this incident of suffering returns to influence you, revisit it again in the same manner until you can let go of it.

- Sometimes in recalling and trying to heal past hurts, we feel anger toward our Creator for letting bad things happen or for not preventing them. If this is the case with you, open a dialog with God. Do not be afraid to say exactly all that is in your soul. Think of Job's harsh words to his Creator, an example of the great biblical tradition of addressing lamentations to God. Remember, at the end, God championed Job and will champion you, too.

To strengthen you for the outer mission, seek the help you need in soul healing or soul making from the Source of all healing.

DAY 3

Tension Between Missions

Many Christian missionaries use as their banner, "To Win the World for Christ." Those of us who are not anointed to be church missionaries heading to exotic lands may wonder how we, in our own way, can win the world for Christ. For instance, a vocation to a scientific discipline has not usually been understood to be missionary work. Thus, scientists might feel that they have two missions: one, to study nature, and the other, to win the world for Christ. The connection between the two missions may seem nonexistent or tenuous at best.

Probably the most common solution is to compartmentalize the time spent on each mission, sometimes wondering which ought to take precedence, sometimes feeling guilty about involvement in the "worldly" occupation. Teilhard, the scientist, made this observation:

> I do not think I am exaggerating when I say that nine out of ten practicing Christians feel that man's work is always at the level of a 'spiritual encumbrance.' In spite of the practice of right intentions, and the day offered every morning to God, the general run of the faithful dimly feel that time spent at the office or the studio, in the fields or in the factory, is time diverted from prayer and adoration. . . . It is impossible, too, to aim at the deep religious life reserved for those who have the leisure to pray or preach all day long. A few moments of the day can be salvaged for God, yes, but the best hours are absorbed, or at any rate cheapened, by material cares. Under the sway of this feeling, large numbers of Catholics lead a double or crippled life in practice: they have to step out of their human dress so as to have faith in themselves as Christians—and inferior Christians at that. (*The Divine Milieu*, p. 34)

Teilhard conceived of a meeting and joining with God in all work activity in the world. He argued against the notion of two missions—one for Sunday and one for weekdays. He maintained that we have a single mission: we draw nearer to God through the details of any sort of work that furthers an ongoing creation.

> There was reason to fear . . . that the seeking after, and expectation of, the Kingdom of Heaven might deflect human activity from its natural tasks, or at least entirely eclipse any interest in them. . . . The conjunction of God and the world has just taken place under our eyes in the domain of action. No, God does not deflect our gaze prematurely from the work He Himself has given us, since He presents Himself to us as attainable through that very work. Nor does He blot out, in His intense light, the detail of our earthly aims, since the intimacy of our union with Him is in fact a function of the exact fulfilment of the least of our tasks. We ought to accustom ourselves to this basic truth till we are steeped in it, until it becomes as familiar to us as the perception of relief or the reading of words. God, in all that is most living and incarnate in Him, is not withdrawn from us beyond the tangible sphere; He is waiting for us at every moment in our action, in our work of the moment. He is in some sort at the tip of my pen, my spade, my brush, my needle—of my heart and of my thought. (*The Divine Milieu*, p. 33)

- Reread Teilhard's ponderings. Let these words lead your thoughts where they will. Spend some time with your reactions.
- Make two columns on a page. In the left-hand column, list all your daily activities that might be considered worldly occupations. In the right-hand column, write your reflections about how God waits in each activity or how each activity can make you a partner with God in the process of cocreation.

Converse with the ever present God about any disconnections you feel between your work and God's work. Ask God how to heal any tensions you feel between the two.

DAY 4

Go Forth

Worship services almost always end with a form of dismissal, a sending forth of nourished and blessed, revived and re-inspired Christians into the world to go about God's work there:

"*Ite, missa est.*"

"Go, the mass is ended."

"Depart in peace."

"Depart! The Spirit of the Lord go with you unto eternal life!"

"Let us go forth, rejoicing in the power of the Spirit."

"Go forth to love and serve the Lord."

Concerning the dismissal from worship, Teilhard wrote:

Try, with God's help, to perceive the connection—even physical and natural—which binds your labour with the building of the Kingdom of Heaven; try to realise that heaven itself smiles upon you and, through your works, draws you to itself; then, as you leave church for the noisy streets, you will remain with only one feeling, that of continuing to immerse yourself in God. If your work is dull or exhausting, take refuge in the inexhaustible and becalming interest of progressing in the divine life. If your work enthralls you, then allow the spiritual impulse which matter communicates to you to enter into your taste for God whom you know better and desire more under the veil of His works. Never, at any time, 'whether eating or drinking,' consent to do anything without first of all realising its significance and constructive value *in Christo Jesu,* and pursuing it with all your might. (*The Divine Milieu,* p. 35)

Teilhard's "The Mass on the World" ends with the following passage that serves as a prayer of self-dedication to the work to which he is dismissed:

It is to your body in this its fullest extension—that is, to the world become through your power and my faith the glorious living crucible in which everything melts away in order to be born anew; it is to this that I dedicate myself with all the resources which your creative magnetism has brought forth in me: with the all too feeble resources of my scientific knowledge, with my religious vows, with my priesthood, and (most dear to me) with my deepest human convictions. It is in this dedication, Lord Jesus, I desire to live, in this I desire to die. (*Hymn of the Universe,* p. 31)

The eucharistic worship service is sometimes called the Mass, derived from the Latin words of dismissal, *"Ite, missa est."* What we do in worship should not be incoherent or unintegrated with our mission, our work in the world outside the doors of church.

- Meditate on the "worldly connection," the interface between the gathering in for communal worship and the sending out again into the world.
- Write your own prayer of dismissal, a prayer that you can say when you leave the house in the morning and when you come home from work, to help you realize that your mission continues in all that you do.

Begin a dialog with God about how worship nurtures your mission outside the doors of church and how work can enrich your prayer.

Christ Loves Us First: Yes or No

Consider these premises for Christian mission: God is love; God loves us; our mission in the most general way is to love God through our love for the world and for other people.

Now consider the problem that often blocks our mission: For most of us, accepting God's love is awfully difficult. John's Epistle says, "we love because he first loved us" (1 John 4:19). To accept that we have a sacred mission in the world calls for a spiritual transformation to become more accepting of God's love for us so that we can feel that we are actually cocreators and highly valued as such by God.

Medieval English mystic Julian of Norwich experienced a series of revelations, the fruit of which was her unshakable conviction that God does love us. She said:

> In our making, God almighty is our loving Father, and God all wisdom is our loving Mother, with the love and the goodness of the Holy Spirit, which is all one God, one Lord. . . . He says: I love you and you love me, and our love will never divide in two. (*Showings*, pp. 293–294)

Although God's love dwells with us, we often need to clean the windows of the soul to see this love. Teresa of Ávila used a particular meditation to allow herself to experience Christ's love for her. She frequently recommended it to those under her direction.

- Sit quietly. Relax. Then imagine that Jesus is standing right in front of you, gazing at you.

    Look back at him. Teresa says to simply pay attention and notice that Jesus is gazing at you lovingly and humbly.

    Notice once again that he looks at you lovingly and humbly.

    Hold Jesus' gaze as long as you can. Invite his love and admiration to flow into your soul. Let go of any feelings of unworthiness or embarrassment. They do not come to you from Jesus.

■ Compose a litany of thanksgiving for all the signs of God's love for you. After each gift, say, "I thank you God for this sign of your love. May it invite me to love what you love, myself, my neighbor, and my world."

Offer this prayer of Teresa of Ávila:
>Let nothing trouble you,
>Let nothing scare you,
>All is fleeting,
>God alone is unchanging.
>Patience
>Everything obtains.
>Who possesses God
>Nothing wants.
>God alone suffices.

>Nada te turbe,
>Nada te espante,
>Todo se pasa,
>Dios no se muda,
>La Paciencia
>Todo lo alcanza;
>Quien a Dios tiene
>Nada le falta.
>Sólo Dios basta.

(*The Collected Works of St. Teresa of Ávila*, p. 386)

DAY 6

Return

Mission and return are parts of a cycle. The story of the mission of the seventy in the Gospel of Luke continues:

> The seventy returned with joy, saying, "Lord, in your name even the demons submit to us!" He said to them, "I watched Satan fall from heaven like a flash of lightning. See, I have given you authority to tread on snakes and scorpions, and over all the power of the enemy; and nothing will hurt you. Nevertheless, do not rejoice at this, that the spirits submit to you, but rejoice that your names are written in heaven." (Luke 10:17–20)

We go out to work, to do the mission that Christ gave us. But we gain new insight into our mission when we return to Christ with it, again and again.

■ What stories of your work week do you bring back to Jesus? Some may even include "snakes and scorpions." What stories do you censor—as being too mundane or too secular—or because you think they show you in a bad light? Consider each story of the last week.

As he listens to your stories, Jesus looks on you lovingly and humbly. He turns away for a moment to get water and a towel—to wash your feet after your travels. Imagine yourself with him. Hear his thanks to you for your labors this week on behalf of the City of God. Notice that he is preparing to send you out again after he has washed you and fed you. Join him fully in your imagination.

Request from God the graces you need to understand this past week of work and the graces you need to do your mission in the coming week.

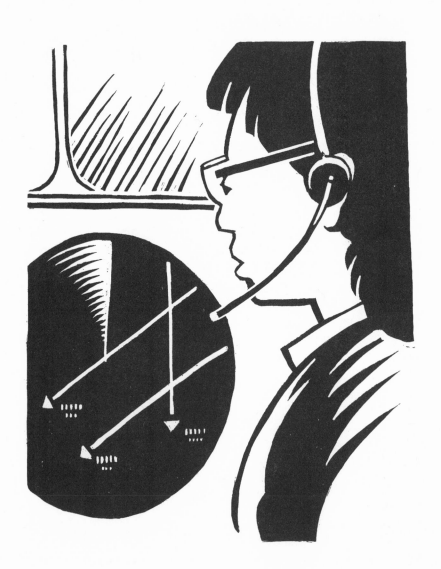

Success

In our working life, what keeps most of us going is the satisfaction derived from successes great and small: projects completed, admiration of peers, new discoveries, elegant results, recognitions, publications, and so on. The high times of success confirm our choice of vocation. The memories of them are reassuring during the middling and low times.

It is important to be aware of God's joy during these times of success, of God's pride in our work as a partner in ongoing cocreation. This week's exercises offer opportunities to reflect on the successes of your work, their significance to you and to your career, and their significance to God.

DAY 1

Success and Survival of the Fittest

After the publication of Charles Darwin's *On the Origin of Species* in 1859, the concept of evolution found widespread application in many fields other than biology. For example, stars and galaxies evolve; personalities evolve, languages evolve, neighborhoods evolve, economies evolve, and civilizations evolve.

The most persistent misunderstanding and misapplication of the notion of evolution is in the belief that competition among people within a society leads to "the survival of the fittest." The evolution of a "better" human species is served whenever poorer, slower, weaker human specimens are conquered, marginalized, or eliminated. This is the reasoning of social Darwinism. It became part of Nazi belief. For social Darwinists, success, measured in terms of money and power, is nature's reward for the fittest: the smartest, the worthiest—the winners.

The most dangerous ideas arise when social Darwinism is given a theological underpinning. Such theologies legitimate ruthless economic and political competition, claiming that success goes not just to the fittest, but to those whom God favors. The accumulation of wealth and power becomes sacramental, an outward and visible sign of the inward grace of divine favor. Such theologies found great popularity during Teilhard's lifetime. Here is a brief passage he wrote on the subject:

> As a paleontologist I cannot preserve any illusion about the fact and the inexorable forms of biological competition. But, in the same capacity, I absolutely reject a crude transference of the mechanical laws of selection to the domain of man. For if nature teaches us plainly that there is a universal struggle for life, she teaches us no less categorically that in passing from one level of existence to another living properties can subsist only by being transformed or transposed. Mutual exploitation and destruction may be the necessary condition between infra-human groups since they live by continually supplanting one another and breaking away

from one another [to become new species]. The case of the human "bundle" is quite opposite. If, following our theory, it can progress only by converging, hostile competition must be replaced within man by brotherly emulation, and war becomes meaningless except in relation to dangers and conquests external to mankind as a whole. (*Letters from a Traveller*, p. 268)

Social Darwinism creeps into our thinking in subtle forms at one time or another. Perhaps it has found its way into our understanding of success in our work and of God's action in our life.

- Spend some time sorting out the meaning of success for you. Compose a list of characteristics you use to signify success. Remember: be ruthlessly honest, naming your real criteria, not what you think should be the criteria for success.

    Review your list, asking, Would Christ Jesus measure success by my criteria?

- Now list some criteria for success that you believe Christ would use.

Converse with God about the role of success in your image of yourself and in the shaping of your work.

The Great Endeavor

If we have difficulty recognizing and claiming the successes of our work, it often helps to look at how they have assisted in realizing God's hopes for the world. For example, Teilhard believed that we are called to master natural forces in order to put them to better use for the world's benefit. The language of domination dates the expression of his views, certainly, but still, his grand view of cooperating with God urged him to excellence in his work. Teilhard committed himself wholeheartedly to increasing, as he says, "the divine atmosphere":

> Then it is really true, Lord? By helping in the spread of science and freedom I can increase the density of the divine atmosphere, in itself as well as for me, that atmosphere in which it is always my one desire to be immersed. By laying hold on the earth I enable myself to cling closely to you.
>
> May the kingdom of matter, then, under our scrutinies and our manipulations, surrender to us the secrets of its texture, its movements, its history.
>
> May the world's energies, mastered by us, bow down before us and accept the yoke of our power.
>
> May the race of men, grown to fuller consciousness and greater strength, become grouped into rich and happy organisms in which life shall be put to better use and bring in a hundredfold return.
>
> May the universe offer to our gaze the symbols and the forms of all harmony and all beauty.
>
> I must *search:* and I must *find.*
>
> What is at stake, Lord, is the element wherein you will dwell here on earth.
>
> What is at stake is your existence amongst us. (*Hymn of the Universe,* pp. 117–118)

Notice that Teilhard's theological metaphor is one of human and divine cooperation in the creative process. This vision is an alternative to the idea that humans must struggle to discern and obey the will of a God who remains hidden and removed from worldly occupations. By involvement in and with the world, learning more and more about its workings, we come into a deeper relationship with the Creator. To Teilhard, that is success.

- Read Teilhard's words again and recall some of your own successes that seem most clearly related to God's work in the world.
- Ponder the role your work has in creating harmony and beauty in the world.

Pray these words of Teilhard's: "By helping in the spread of science and freedom I can increase the density of the divine atmosphere." Substitute the name of your work for "the spread of science." Feel how the prayer sounds. Then talk with God about your success in increasing the density of the divine atmosphere.

Return to an Earlier Meditation

Perhaps one of the earlier exercises is begging for more prayerful thought. Or perhaps you wish to reflect on a related or different topic. This space provides the invitation and opportunity to read and write further.

→) Discerning where you are and staying on the path to where you want to go. —

DAY 4

Humility or Humiliation?

In our various Christian traditions, most of us have been drilled in exercises meant to encourage humility as a virtue. These exercises probably instilled more humiliation than humility, taking their toll on our confidence and our ability to see our successes for what they are. Some of these lessons told us to view ourselves as God's little children—not grown children, but little children—utterly dependent upon God's omnipotence.

Teilhard turned this whole notion upside down, saying that God depends utterly on us, God's people, to extend the work begun by the divine hand. This view goes a long way in restoring our respect for ourselves and our work: God needs us to do the work of divinizing the world, sanctifying it, and building the Reign of God. The process is one of supernatural evolution. In Teilhard's view and that of other leading scientists of his generation, creation reached its pinnacle in Homo sapiens through natural evolution and the drive to survive and bear progeny. Supernatural evolution, on the other hand, is a human enterprise, a reaching for God in Christ, a convergence of humanity and divinized nature upon a point of unity in God, called the "Omega Point." This convergence is powered not by the will to survive and procreate, but by the united human will to love.

Teilhard wrote extensively about this metaphysical idea. It preoccupied him in his later years, and he intended to look for scientific evidence of the convergence. The following moving passage is taken from the epilogue of *The Divine Milieu*:

> The progress of the universe, and in particular of the human universe, does not take place in competition with God, nor does it squander energies that we rightly owe to Him. The greater man becomes, the more humanity becomes united, with consciousness of, and mastery of, its potentialities, the more beautiful creation will be, the more perfect adoration will become, and the more Christ will find, for mystical extensions, a body worthy of resurrection. The world can no

more have two summits than a circumference can have two centres. The star for which the world is waiting, without yet being able to give it a name, or rightly appreciate its true transcendence, or even recognise the most spiritual and divine of its rays, is, necessarily, Christ Himself, in whom we hope. To desire the Parousia, all we have to do is to let the very heart of the earth, as we Christianise it, beat within us. (P. 137)

The virtue of humility means seeing the truth about our authentic place in the scheme of creation. Yes, we depend on God for our being. God holds us in the divine embrace. In God we live and move and have our being. However, as Teilhard believed, we become God's hands, eyes, ears, and voice in bringing all things into sacred unity. Thus, God invites us to celebrate the occasions when we promote such unity.

- Meditate on this image from Teilhard's words: "The greater man becomes, the more humanity becomes united, . . . the more beautiful creation will be, the more perfect adoration will become." Ask yourself: How am I succeeding in becoming a "greater" person, in uniting human beings?
- Perform some simple ritual to celebrate your growth into a fuller humanity.

Ask for the gift to be able to discern more fully how your own life has contributed to "the progress of the universe" as it becomes for Christ "a body worthy of resurrection."

DAY 5

Apostles of Success

Since the early days of Christianity, different interpretations of the Gospels have been taught. Understanding the nature of Christ's victory or success and the nature of salvation have been particularly problematic.

In his First Epistle to the Corinthians, Paul makes several references to the teachings of other missionaries, such as Apollos. It seems that they proclaimed a Gospel message about Christ's success that was different from the one taught by Paul.

The message of these rival evangelists appealed particularly to the Greeks because it downplayed the significance of the cross in discipleship. The message was triumphalist in its claim that Christ's followers were immortal and living in the success of resurrection right now, their spirits having been delivered from bondage to flesh. Spiritual gifts, especially the ability to speak in tongues, apparently provided sufficient proof for them of resurrection already achieved. With this ultimate success, these rival evangelists claimed that it didn't matter what sort of selfish, even debauched, lives Christians led.

Paul expended considerable effort trying to correct the error of this message of success that so impressed the Christian community at Corinth, and which persists in its appeal even today among certain Christian groups. In this magnificent passage, Paul summarizes his teaching about the true gifts of the Spirit:

> If I speak in the tongues of mortals and of angels, but do not have love, I am a noisy gong or a clanging cymbal. And if I have prophetic powers, and understand all mysteries and all knowledge, and if I have all faith, so as to remove mountains, but do not have love, I am nothing. If I give away all my possessions, and if I hand over my body so that I may boast, but do not have love, I gain nothing.
>
> Love is patient; love is kind; love is not envious or boastful or arrogant or rude. It does not insist on its own way; it is not irritable or resentful; it does not rejoice in wrongdoing,

but rejoices in the truth. It bears all things, believes all things, hopes all things, endures all things.

Love never ends. But as for prophecies, they will come to an end; as for tongues, they will cease; as for knowledge, it will come to an end. For we know only in part, and we prophesy only in part; but when the complete comes, the partial will come to an end. When I was a child, I spoke like a child, I thought like a child, I reasoned like a child; when I became an adult, I put an end to childish ways. For now we see in a mirror, dimly, but then we will see face to face. Now I know only in part; then I will know fully, even as I have been fully known. And now faith, hope, and love abide, these three; and the greatest of these is love. (1 Corinthians 13)

Simply put, for Christians success means love, hope, and faith.

- Meditate upon the importance, for yourself, your congregation, and the whole church, of Paul's words concerning success in 1 Corinthians, chapter 13.
- Ponder this phrase from Paul over and over, letting its specific message for you become clear: "If I speak in the tongues of mortals and of angels, but do not have love, I am a noisy gong or a clanging cymbal."

Ask the Holy Spirit to fill your heart and your work with love, hope, and faith: the soul of Christian success.

The Success of Palm Sunday

Read Matthew's account of Jesus' entry into Jerusalem. Find your place in the scene. How old are you as you join the story? Are you a disciple, a stranger, or perhaps even the one riding the donkey? Hear the voices, the reproachful ones and the hopeful ones. Smell the people, the animals, the other scents in the air. Feel the weather and the atmosphere, the excitement of the holiday mixed with the violation of the place by Roman occupation. What do you think is going on here, and who is this celebrated personage?

> Jesus sent two disciples, saying to them, "Go into the village ahead of you, and immediately you will find a donkey tied, and a colt with her; untie them and bring them to me. . . . The disciples went and did as Jesus had directed them; they brought the donkey and the colt, and put their cloaks on them, and he sat on them. A very large crowd spread their cloaks on the road, and others cut branches from the trees and spread them on the road. The crowds that went ahead of him and that followed were shouting,
> "Hosanna to the Son of David!
>   Blessed is the one who comes in the name of the Lord!
>   Hosanna in the highest heaven!"
> When he entered Jerusalem, the whole city was in turmoil, asking, "Who is this?" (Matthew 21:1–10)

What sort of a success story do you think this is? A small-town rabbi hits the big city and makes the big time. However, as people experienced Jesus in different ways, they offered different answers to the question, "Who is this?"

Maybe our success as Christians is not greeted with a procession through the streets, but then many of those who shouted "Hosanna" probably shouted "Crucify him" some time later. Of all the strands we may be "braiding" in our life's activities at any one time, we may consider one or two particular strands to be the most important to the success of God's work in the world.

Hindsight often shows us that God selected some other strand to embellish. The fleeting "hosannas" of others should remind us of our need for God's grace, even as we celebrate the successes God has led us to.

- What aspects of your way of life, your work, your relationships would Jesus say "Hosanna" about if you were being brought in procession through Jerusalem?
- Does some event, considered a success in your life and work, take on new meaning in light of this story of Jesus' day in the "hosannas"?

Give thanks to God for the graces that have strengthened you and have led to your success in building the holy City of God.

Setbacks

Everyone, no matter how successful, experiences professional setbacks and personal diminishments. For some people, getting established in their vocation seems a constant uphill struggle. Certainly, gender, racial, and ethnic bias in the scientific and business communities and elsewhere have taken a heavy personal toll, and they continue to do so. Setbacks can be so severe that the frustration colors other areas of our life.

We tend to organize our life into more or less segregated spheres of activity: family, social, religious, professional, and so on. The weakness of this model becomes obvious when we find ourselves unable to keep going like automatons at the office, or at home when someone close is stricken with illness or an accident.

To the degree that we are whole and integrated persons, our losses in one sphere will make their effects felt in all other spheres of our life.

The exercises for this week invite you to recall the setbacks that have affected you and your vocation. Before rushing to recall and express the possible redemptive value of these setbacks, allow yourself to express the discouragement and sense of loss as you remember them. Block the "it's all for the best" reflex, pausing first to offer to God the whole constellation of your emotions. Finally, then, allow yourself to ponder the gains from these setbacks, seen with the perspective of faithful hindsight.

Jesus Began to Cry

When John the Evangelist composed his Gospel, he allowed Judea to symbolize the place of diminishment, associating it with sickness, death, darkness, and blindness. As you read the following story, notice the language of diminishment.

Now there was a man named Lazarus who was sick; he was from Bethany, the village of Mary and her sister Martha. . . . So the sisters sent to inform Jesus, "Lord, the one whom you love is sick." But when Jesus heard it, he said,

"This sickness is not to end in death;
rather it is for God's glory,
that the Son [of God] may be glorified through it."

. . . And so, even when he heard that Lazarus was sick, he stayed on where he was two days longer.

Then, at last, Jesus said to the disciples, "Let us go back to Judea." "Rabbi," protested the disciples, "the Jews were just now trying to stone you, and you are going back up there again?" Jesus answered,

"Are there not twelve hours of daylight?
If [people go] walking by day, [they do] not stumble
because [they] can see the light of this world.
But if [they go] walking at night, [they] will stumble
because [they have] no light in [them]."

He made this remark, and then, later, he told them, "Our beloved Lazarus has fallen asleep, but I am going there to wake him up." At this the disciples objected, "If he has fallen asleep, Lord, his life will be saved." . . . So finally Jesus told them plainly, "Lazarus is dead. And I am happy for your sake that I was not there so that you may come to have faith. In any event, let us go to him." . . .

When Jesus arrived, he found that Lazarus had [already] been four days in the tomb. Now Bethany was not far from Jerusalem, just under two miles; and many of the Jews had come out to offer sympathy to Martha and Mary because of their brother. When Martha heard that Jesus was coming, she went to meet him, while Mary sat quietly at home. Martha said to Jesus, "Lord, if you had been here, my brother would never have died. Even now, I am sure that whatever you ask of God, God will give you." "Your brother will rise again," Jesus assured her. "I know he will rise again," Martha replied, "in the resurrection on the last day." Jesus told her,

"I am the resurrection [and the life]:
[those] who believe in me,
even if [they] die will come to life.
And everyone who is alive and believes in me
shall never die at all.—

Do you believe this?" "Yes, Lord," she replied. "I have come to believe that you are the Messiah, the Son of God, [the one] who is to come into the world."

Now when she had said this, she went off and called her sister Mary. "The Teacher is here and calls for you," she whispered. As soon as Mary heard this, she got up quickly and started out toward him. . . . The Jews who were in the house with Mary, consoling her, saw her get up quickly and go out; and so they followed her, thinking that she was going to the tomb to weep there. When Mary came to the place where Jesus was and saw him, she fell at his feet and said to him, "Lord, if you had been here, my brother would never have died." Now when Jesus saw her weeping, and the Jews who had accompanied her also weeping, he shuddered, moved with the deepest emotions.

"Where have you laid him?" he asked. "Lord, come and see," they told him. Jesus began to cry, and this caused the Jews to remark, "See how much he loved him!" (John 11:1–36, in The Gospel According to John I–XII)

Jesus, God-with-us, suffered, grieved, and wept. He loved people. Their sorrow was his sorrow. Like us, Jesus experienced setbacks. From a human point of view, his death on the cross appears a total disaster, a thorough failure. None of us is immune from changes in plans, bereavement, and pain.

■ Recall from your own experience a time when your itinerary, literal or figurative, was changed, as Jesus' was, by sudden loss. Perhaps you were even called "back to Judea." Imagine sending word to Jesus to come and join you. Imagine him changing his plans to come and weep with you.

■ Ponder a recent loss or setback. Attend to your feelings.

Talk with Jesus about your setbacks, especially any particular setback that you are still grieving over. Ask for the light of grace needed for comprehending the gain hidden in this setback.

Limitations of the Body

Some months after his return from Peking in 1946, Teilhard was offered a new research opportunity: the chance to examine a collection of recently discovered fossils in South Africa. In preparation, he attended to the delicate arrangements of collaboration with professional colleagues and secured the necessary permission and funding for the trip.

On 1 June 1947, just a few weeks before he was scheduled to leave Paris for Johannesburg, Teilhard suffered a heart attack and hovered near death for three weeks. He did recover, and during his convalescence he wrote the following in a letter to his good friend l'Abbé Breuil:

> I have to call on all the philosophy of my faith to make part of myself and put to constructive use what is in itself heartbreaking. Everything was working out so well and was so close to realisation! But thank you all the same for all you've done for me. . . . I don't, in fact, even know the exact name of what I've had (a lesion somewhere round the heart or the coronary arteries). All I have felt has been a sort of rheumatic pain, with attacks of nausea, but no breathlessness. I must have strained myself without realising it, for I had the impression of being in such excellent form. I still can't estimate the extent of the "disaster," that is to say how far extensive field-work will still be possible. If the worst comes to the worst I shall concentrate on mental work. (*Letters from a Traveller*, pp. 293–294)

In the hurry of our life, we may forget the wisdom of the body. Suddenly, like Teilhard's heart attack, some bodily malfunction stops us in our tracks, saying in effect, "Listen up! Pay attention!" Setback? Yes. Opportunity? Definitely.

- Has your own body given you hints, subtle or otherwise, that something in your way of life has been out of balance or unwholesome? Ponder these hints. Engage them in conversation. For instance, write a dialog with some ache or with your sleeplessness. As strange as it may seem initially, your body-self has something to say.
- Have there been instances when your body refused to go along with some plans you had made. How do you feel in the face of such "rebellion"? Attend to this rebellion.

Converse with your Creator about the wonder of your body, any ailments or disharmony in your body-self, and your attentiveness to your body-self.

Limitations of Circumstance

Teilhard's heart condition left him unable to resume the vigorous sort of fieldwork to which he had previously devoted himself. However, in 1948, a year after his heart attack, he was offered an extraordinary professional opportunity when he was nominated for a professorship at the Collège de France. He wrote to l'Abbé Breuil in October, from Rome:

> As the Collège de France kindly approached me about a vacant Chair (to be allotted possibly to prehistory), . . . the Father General decided to have me come here to talk about a number of things at the same time. . . . In a week from today I shall know whether to say yes or no to [the administrator of the Collège] about my candidature—it comes up in November, so it's becoming urgent. . . . Being barred from field-work, as I have been for the last year, makes me less keen, of course, to teach prehistory. On the other hand I find the general question of anthropogenesis more and more interesting and absorbing. It would obviously be a wonderful chance for me to be able, even if only for two years (for that's all it would be), to take advantage of the Collège as a platform. In short, I am feeling quite philosophical about the outcome. I'll keep you posted, of course. (*Letters from a Traveller*, pp. 301–302)

On the last day of his visit to Rome, Teilhard was advised by the Father General of the Society of Jesus not to take the position at the Collège. It is now felt that the recommendation was made not only because the academic subject matter was too controversial, but also because Teilhard would be able to have a platform for expounding his ideas about evolution, in both human and theological terms. At that time, the Roman Catholic church was intensely nervous about the so-called new theology coming particularly from French Jesuits. In faithfulness to the vows of his order, Teilhard decided not to be a candidate for the position.

Whenever Teilhard became discouraged, anxious, or frustrated, his belief in Providence held firm. To his cousin Marguerite, he wrote in 1951 about his exile in New York City:

> Rome seems favourably inclined to the idea of my prolonging my stay here. . . . It will be 1925 over again [when he was exiled to China because of his ideas], with New York instead of China. The only thing is, I'm seventy. . . . Even so, it may be, once more, an intervention of Providence, and the opening up of a new field. (*Letters from a Traveller,* p. 320)

- Does Teilhard's experience remind you of any setbacks in your own life, when circumstances of family, finances, country, church—or something else—forced you or prompted you to choose to let certain exciting opportunities pass by? If memories of sadness and frustration are stirred up, pray them out, inviting God's participation.
- What helps you hold on to faith in the face of setbacks? Where is the source of your hope? Can you say what Teilhard said, "It may be, once more, an intervention of Providence and the opening up of a new field"?

Ask for the grace you need to keep the flames of hope and trust in Providence alive in you.

Return to an Earlier Meditation

If one of the earlier exercises held particular meaning for you, or if your work on one of them feels unfinished, now is a good time to return to it.

One Christian's View of Death

Concerning physical weakness and death, Teilhard wrote an essay entitled "The Passivities of Diminishment." Perhaps his beliefs about the process of death and its meaning may be helpful to you in your own search for meaning.

The moment has come to plumb the decidedly negative side of our existences—the side on which, however far we search, we cannot discern any happy result or any solid conclusion to what happens to us. It is easy enough to understand that God can be grasped in and through every life. But can God also be found in and through every death? This is what disconcerts us. And yet this is what we must learn to recognise habitually and in practice, under pain of remaining blind to what is most specifically Christian in the Christian vision, and under pain, too, of losing contact with the divine on one of the widest and most receptive fronts of our life.

In death, as in an ocean, all our slow or swift diminishments flow out and merge. Death is the sum and consummation of all our diminishments.

. . . We shall find the Christian faith absolutely explicit in its affirmations and practices. Christ has conquered death, not only by suppressing its evil effects, but by reversing its sting. By virtue of the Resurrection, nothing any longer kills inevitably but everything is capable of becoming the blessed touch of the divine hands, the blessed influence of the will of God upon our lives. . . .

Events which show themselves experimentally in our lives as pure loss will become an immediate factor in the union we dream of establishing with Him. . . .

Now the great victory of the Creator and Redeemer, in the Christian vision, is to have transformed what is in itself a universal power of diminishment and extinction into an essentially life-giving factor. God must, in some way or other, make room for Himself, hollowing us out and emptying us, if He is finally to penetrate into us. And in order to as-similate us in Him, He must break the molecules of our be-ing so as to re-cast and re-model us. The function of death is to provide the necessary entrance into our inmost selves. It will make us undergo the required dissociation. It will put us into the state organically needed if the divine fire is to de-scend upon us. And in that way its fatal power to decompose and dissolve will be harnessed to the most sublime opera-tions of life. What was by nature empty and void, a return to plurality, can, in each human existence, become plenitude and unity in God.

O God, . . . when the signs of age begin to mark my body (and still more when they touch my mind); when the ill that is to diminish me or carry me off strikes from without or is born with-in me; when the painful moment comes in which I suddenly awaken to the fact that I am ill or growing old; and above all at that last moment when I feel I am losing hold of myself and am absolutely passive within the hands of the great unknown forces that have formed me; in all those dark moments, O God, grant that I may understand that it is You (provided only my faith is strong enough) who are painfully parting the fibres of my being in order to penetrate to the very marrow of my substance and bear me away within Yourself. (The Divine Milieu, pp. 52–62)

When we embrace the Good News, we also embrace the Gos-pel belief that death is not final. We rise with Christ. So when death comes, we can embrace it, as Teilhard did. Death can be an act of communion.

- Settle yourself comfortably but alertly in a chair. Relax and breathe deeply and slowly. Remind yourself that you are held in God's hands. When you are ready, call to mind any losses you will experience or are experiencing in your dying. Which of these losses causes you the most distress? As you list the losses, which stir the most feelings? Converse with Jesus about these.

- What changes in your relationships, lifestyle, work, and spiri-tuality would lessen regrets at the time of your death? What re-sentments, anger, possessions, and so on, clutter your life? Decide on at least one thing to let go of now. Offer it to God, saying: "Take this, my God. I let go of it as unnecessary. Give me only a desire for your love."

Offer this prayer to the Risen Christ:

May my being, in its self-offering to you, become ever more open and more transparent to your influence!

And may I thus feel your activity coming ever closer, your presence growing ever more intense, everywhere around me.

Fiat, fiat.

(*Hymn of the Universe,* p. 136)

If Teilhard's prayer is not adequate for your needs, pray from your own experience of death and diminishment.

Lazarus, Come Out!

Day 1 of this week's reflections left Jesus in front of the tomb in Judea, weeping with Martha and Mary. But the story continues:

> Some of [the crowd] said, "He opened the eyes of that blind man. Couldn't he also have done something to stop this man from dying?" With this again arousing his emotions, Jesus came to the tomb.
>
> It was a cave with a stone laid across it. "Take away the stone," Jesus ordered. Martha, the dead man's sister, said to him, "Lord, it is four days; by now there must be a stench." Jesus replied, "Didn't I assure you that if you believed, you would see the glory of God?" So they took away the stone. Then Jesus looked upward and said,
>
> "Father, I thank you because you heard me.
>
> Of course, I knew that you always hear me,
>
> but I say it because of the crowd standing around,
>
> that they may believe that you sent me."
>
> Having said this, he shouted in a loud voice, "Lazarus, come out!" The dead man came out, bound hand and foot with linen strips and his face wrapped in a cloth. "Untie him," Jesus told them, "and let him go." (John 11:37–44, in The Gospel According to John I–XII)

The pre-eminent Johannine scholar Raymond E. Brown points out that the Evangelist gives such significance to this miracle as to make it the cause for the convocation of the Sanhedrin that decided upon Jesus' execution. The irony is this: Jesus gives life to people, and people condemn Jesus to death. Even so, faith in Jesus can free us from the "linen strips" that bind us in our fears concerning setbacks, diminishment, and death.

- Can you find a Lazarus symbol among the diminishments you have known? Having "wrapped up" your loss and laid it to rest, have you ever experienced Jesus asking you to reopen the closed tomb (or closed chapter), so that he could call Lazarus out again, still quite viable? "Untie him and let him go."

Ask the Risen Christ to help you untie and let go of any fears you have about diminishment and death.

Week 6

Transformation and Transfiguration

The discovery of the ultimate good or purpose for one's work, especially for vocational successes and setbacks, can be an experience of tremendous power. People often identify such a discovery as a catalyst for the deepening of religious faith or even for conversion. They may find a new dimension or direction to their work. They may say that their eyes have been opened in some new way. The labor of searching for and working out the meaning of experience is surely the work of transformation or transfiguration that we share with God.

Spend prayerful time this week recalling the transformative work you and God have done and still need to do in your life and vocation. In Teilhard's thought, human labors are transformed and used by God in the evolution of the noosphere, an approximate equivalent to the biblical term, City or Reign of God. The noosphere emerges through the physical and intellectual work of human beings, with God overseeing the architecture. The model of evolution was borrowed and adapted from the field of geology, the scientific discipline in which Teilhard was trained. The term *noosphere* describes the next level of geological and biological evolution, the domain of the *nous,* the Greek term for mind or intellect. (The biosphere is the sphere or domain of all living things, which in turn evolved from the nonliving rocky geosphere, watery hydrosphere, and atmosphere.)

During this week's meditations, consider the vocabulary of your own work life, and try to use it, as Teilhard did, to describe your vocational partnership with God in transformation and transfiguration.

DAY 1

Our Heart Burning Within Us

The following account of an appearance of the resurrected Christ to two disciples reminds us that the meaning and purpose of Jesus' death were not immediately apparent to most of his followers. Such understanding grew slowly, with much prayer, Scripture study, and earnest discussion among disciples, as they continued in their everyday, worldly occupations. As you read the story, try to put yourself into the scene:

Now on that same day two [of Jesus' disciples] were going to a village called Emmaus, about seven miles from Jerusalem, and talking with each other about all these things that had happened. While they were talking and discussing, Jesus himself came near and went with them, but their eyes were kept from recognizing him. And he said to them, "What are you discussing with each other while you walk along?" They stood still, looking sad. Then one of them, whose name was Cleopas, answered him, "Are you the only stranger in Jerusalem who does not know the things that have taken place there in these days?" He asked them, "What things?" They replied, "The things about Jesus of Nazareth, who was a prophet mighty in deed and word before God and all the people, and how our chief priests and leaders handed him over to be condemned to death and crucified him. But we had hoped that he was the one to redeem Israel. Yes, and besides all this, it is now the third day since these things took place. Moreover, some women of our group astounded us. They were at the tomb early this morning, and when they did not find his body there, they came back and told us that they had indeed seen a vision of angels who said that he was alive. Some of those who were with us went to the tomb and found it just as the women had said; but they did not see him." Then he said to them, "O how foolish you are, and how slow of heart to believe all that the prophets have declared! Was it not necessary that the Messiah should suffer these things and then enter into his glory?" Then beginning with Moses and all the prophets, he interpreted to them the things about himself in all the scriptures.

As they came near the village to which they were going, he walked ahead as if he were going on. But they urged him strongly, saying, "Stay with us, because it is almost evening and the day is now nearly over." So he went in to stay with them. When he was at the table with them, he took the bread, blessed and broke it, and gave it to them. Then their eyes were opened, and they recognized him; and he vanished from their sight. They said to each other, "Were not our hearts burning within us while he was talking to us on the road, while he was opening the scriptures to us?"

That same hour they got up and returned to Jerusalem; and they found the eleven and their companions gathered together. They were saying, "The Lord has risen indeed, and he has appeared to Simon!" Then they told what had happened on the road, and how he had been made known to them in the breaking of the bread. (Luke 24:13–35)

At the time this story was writen, the meaning and purpose of Jesus' death had not been as fully discovered and worked out as it would be when John's Gospel was written. And now, two millennia later, much more praying, studying, discussing, "walking," and "breaking of the bread" has led Christians still further into revelation. Perhaps the evolution of meaning is never complete.

- Read the account again. Pray over the story, setting the scene and entering it yourself. Listen as Jesus speaks. Invite him to dine with you. Let your eyes be opened. Run to tell the other followers the Good News.
- Have you ever encountered Life on your walk "about seven miles" from death? Did you have companions who shared the experience, or were you alone? What changes resulted from the encounter?

Ask Christ for the graces you need to have your eyes opened and to recognize his presence in the world around you.

DAY 2

Hope for the Future

In the last chapter of his popular book on cosmogenesis, *The First Three Minutes,* Nobel laureate and physicist Steven Weinberg reflects on the meaning of his findings with a pessimism that has modeled for many people a "correct" attitude for members of an advanced scientific culture to have. Weinberg writes that whichever way the cosmos ends—expanding and cooling off forever or eventually contracting and collapsing into a cosmic fireball:

> There is not much of comfort in any of this. It is almost irresistible for humans to believe that we have some special relation to the universe, that human life is not just a more-or-less farcical outcome of a chain of accidents reaching back to the first three minutes. . . . It is very hard to realize that this [comfortable planet] is just a tiny part of an overwhelmingly hostile universe. . . . The more the universe seems comprehensible, the more it also seems pointless.
>
> . . . The effort to understand the universe is one of the very few things that lifts human life a little above the level of farce, and gives it some of the grace of tragedy. (Pp. 154–155)

Many people, even Christians, are haunted by the suspicion that Weinberg may be right. An alternative view is the Christian hope for the future, based in the faith that the universe is not hostile to us nor merely indifferent, but is in fact benevolent toward us because of God's very presence within it. This faith is rooted in the communally treasured and validated revelations of God in Scripture, principally the Easter revelation, as well as in the mystical experiences of the saints.

Teilhard wrote about the transformation in vision that happens for those who "dare to believe":

> Though the phenomena of the lower world remain the same—the material determinisms, the vicissitudes of chance, the laws of labor, the agitations of men, the footfalls of death—he who *dares* to believe reaches a sphere of created

94

reality in which things, while retaining their habitual texture, seem to be made out of a different substance. Everything remains the same so far as phenomena are concerned, but at the same time everything becomes luminous, animated, loving. . . .

Through the workings of faith, Christ appears, Christ is born, without any violation of nature's laws, in the heart of the world. (*Hymn of the Universe,* p. 143)

Many staunchly religious people take on Weinberg's position at some time or another, even if only momentarily. Especially during setbacks, his pessimism seems realistic. On the other hand, faith urges us to believe as Teilhard does. Catastrophic events in creation occur, but we can still believe in God's goodness and healing presence. Ultimately, we choose.

- Have you ever been tempted to view the cosmos as pointless, even absurd? If so, remember this period. Whether it comes and goes in momentary flashes or comes during a certain period of your life, what draws you back to Christ?
- Think about the times when your own daring to believe has revealed the light, life, and love in the cosmos. If you are moved to do so, imagine a dialog with Steven Weinberg and offer some words of wisdom to him and other pessimists who are overly impressed with scientific findings.

Ask God for the courage to always "dare to believe."

Day 3

Love of the Here and Now

One source of tension between faith and science has been what many see as the church's excessive orientation toward the future, or its otherworldliness, combined with a disparagement of involvement with this life on earth. Always looking "to the east" for the return of Christ and emphasizing the primacy of life after death, the church has often shown a preference for those scriptural verses that advocate detachment from the world.

We live with many unfortunate results of this emphasis, such as the marginalization of prophetic voices for justice and peace, the careless consumption of environmental resources, an overemphasis upon God's transcendence, neglect of the ramifications of the Incarnation, and, of course, the instillation of guilt in those who claim a vocation in worldly occupations.

We usually read the following familiar selections from the Christian Testament with our "church ears." As you read them this time, pay particular attention to what they are really saying about personal involvement in the here and now, the physical world of our daily life.

> "Do not store up for yourselves treasures on earth, where moth and rust consume and where thieves break in and steal; but store up for yourselves treasures in heaven." (Matthew 6:19–20)

> "I have given them your word, and the world has hated them because they do not belong to the world, just as I do not belong to the world." (John 17:14)

> Religion that is pure and undefiled before God . . . is this: to care for orphans and widows in their distress, and to keep oneself unstained by the world. (James 1:27)

> Adulterers! Do you not know that friendship with the world is enmity with God? Therefore whoever wishes to be a friend of the world becomes an enemy of God. (James 4:4)

But our citizenship is in heaven, and it is from there that we are expecting a Savior, the Lord Jesus Christ. He will transform the body of our humiliation that it may be conformed to the body of his glory. (Philippians 3:20–21)

Teilhard was dismayed by otherworldly emphases that involved an implied disparagement or devaluation of the world that we know and love. His eye also was on the future, but a future that evolves directly from the here and now, where God's Reign is being built through the work of those developing themselves to the fullest in their various vocations. Under the influence of a force of divine attraction, the here and now is proceeding inexorably toward its Omega Point, its fulfillment in Christ:

And since the time when Jesus was born, when He finished growing and died and rose again, *everything has continued to move because Christ has not yet completed His own forming.* He has not yet gathered in to Himself the last folds of the Garment of flesh and love which His disciples are making for him. *The mystical Christ has not yet attained His full growth.* . . . Christ is the Fulfilment even of the natural evolution of beings. (Teilhard de Chardin, *The Future of Man,* p. 305)

- Have you been influenced by the otherworldly, or next-life, emphasis in the Christian church? If so, how? Does this focus help or hinder your mission or calling in life?
- Are you ready to envision your own daily work among the folds of Christ's "Garment of flesh and love"? What does this notion of Teilhard's mean for you?

Converse with Christ about your feelings around Teilhard's phrase, "The mystical Christ has not yet attained His full growth."

DAY 4

Transfiguration, Not Conservation

After the Second World War, Teilhard watched the frustratingly slow proceedings at the Peace Conference. Incorporated into his own Christian hope for the future were his scientific findings as a geobiologist. These findings supported for him a belief in continued evolution of the human species toward "psychic unification" in peace, or "unanimisation."

He thought that evil was served by the inertia that conserved the old, fractured order. Evil encouraged resistance to the development of community and the transfiguration of the human warring impulse. As you read his commentary below, try to identify within yourself the elements of conservative inertia, as well as the elements of transfigurative impetus.

Peace therefore is certain: it is only a matter of time. Inevitably, with an inevitability which is nothing but the supreme expression of liberty, we are moving laboriously and self-critically towards it. But what exactly do we mean by this—*what kind of peace?* . . . A sustained state of growing convergence and concentration, a great organised endeavour. . . . This means that all hope of bourgeois tranquillity, the dreams of "millennary" felicity in which we may be tempted to indulge, must be washed out, eliminated from our horizon. A perfectly-ordered society with everyone living in effortless ease within a fixed framework, a world in a state of tranquil repose, all this has nothing to do with our advancing Universe, apart from the fact that it would rapidly induce a state of deadly tedium. Although, as I believe, concord must of necessity eventually prevail on earth, it can by our premises only take the form of some sort of tense cohesion pervaded and inspired with the same energies, now become harmonious, which were previously wasted in bloodshed. . . . In short, true peace, the only kind that is biologically possible, betokens neither the ending nor the reverse of warfare, but war in a naturally sublimated form. It reflects and corresponds to the normal state of Mankind become at last alive to the possibilities and demands of its evolution.

And here a last question arises, bringing us to the heart of the problem. Why is it, finally, that men are still so painfully incapable of agreeing among themselves; why does the threat of war still appear so menacing? Is it not because they have still not purged themselves sufficiently of the demon of immobilism? Is not the underlying antagonism which separates them at the conference tables quite simply the eternal conflict between motion and inertia, the cleavage between one part of the world that moves and another that does not seek to advance? Let us not forget that faith in peace is not possible, not justifiable, except in a world dominated by faith in the future, *faith in Man* and the progress of Man.

When I look for reassurance as to our future, I do not turn to official utterances, or 'pacifist' manifestations, or conscientious objectors. I turn instinctively towards the ever more numerous institutions and associations of men where in the search for knowledge a new spirit is silently taking shape around us—the soul of Mankind resolved at all costs to achieve, in its total integrity, the uttermost fulfilment of its powers and its destiny. (*The Future of Man*, pp. 153–154)

Faith in the future, faith in humanity's progress, and faith in the Creator all lead to expansion of the soul, and the opening of the heart, mind, and will to all that gives life.

- Are there any forces in your life right now that encourage you to the "uttermost fulfilment" of your powers and destiny? Name these forces and ponder how you can embrace their support more fully.
- Are there any forces of inertia in your life that tell you to hunker down, to protect what you have, to stay disengaged, or to not stick your neck out? Name these forces and ponder how God's grace can liberate you from them.

Talk with Holy Wisdom about embracing the spirit of life, celebrating all that is positive.

Courage for Change

Drawing redemptive value out of experiences of diminishment requires conversion: a fresh vision and the will to change old habits—even instincts. Teilhard wrote of the need for the collective sublimation of the instinct for war making, if humanity, newly possessed of the atomic bomb, was to have a future. Those of us who have lived in families that required massive denial to hold them together need to break out of old familiar patterns in order to find the life that God wants for us. Habitual pain and diminishment become so commonplace that they even feel comfortable in their familiarity.

Read the following prayer and meditate upon the meaning of "the uncharted ocean of charity" in your own life and work, and the courage you require to venture forth onto it.

> No, Lord, you do not ask of me anything that is false or beyond my power to achieve. Through your self-revealing and the power of your grace you simply compel what is most human in us to become at long last aware of itself. Humanity has been sleeping—and still sleeps—lulled within the narrowly confining joys of its little closed loves. In the depths of the human multitude there slumbers an immense spiritual power which will manifest itself only when we have learned how to *break through the dividing walls* of our egoism and raise ourselves up to an entirely new perspective, so that habitually and in a practical fashion we fix our gaze on the universal realities.
>
> Lord Jesus, you who are the Savior of our human activity because you bring us a motive for acting, and the Savior of our human pain because you endow it with a life-giving value: be also the Savior of our human unity by compelling us to repudiate all our pettiness and, relying on you, to venture forth on to the uncharted ocean of charity. (*Hymn of the Universe*, pp. 136–137)

- How have you been "lulled within the narrowly confining joys of [your] little closed loves"? What "pettiness" do you want to repudiate? Do an unsparing inventory with Christ at your side to help.
- With faith in God's constant grace and a clear sense of your own strengths and gifts, how do you want to "venture forth on to the uncharted ocean of charity"?

Ask for the courage that you need to embark on the adventure of charity in the context of your life right now.

DAY 6

A New Door Opening

If Evolution were to reach its highest point, in our small, separate lives, then indeed the enormous travail of terrestrial organisation into which we are born would be no more than a tragic irrelevance. We should all be dupes. We should do better in that case to stop, to call a halt, destroy the machines, close the laboratories, and seek whatever way of escape we can find in pure pleasure or pure nirvana.

But if on the contrary Man sees a new door opening above him, a new stage for his development; if each of us can believe that he is working so that the Universe may be raised, in him and through him, to a higher level—then a new spring of energy will well forth in the heart of Earth's workers. The whole great human organism, overcoming a momentary hesitation, will draw its breath and press on with strength renewed. (*The Future of Man,* pp. 117–118)

For the past forty days, guided reading of the Scriptures and of selections from Teilhard's writing have encouraged a spirituality that integrates God's work and our work in the world. Spirituality, the lived experience of our beliefs, should not be restricted to narrowly "religious" occupations. Teilhard urges the expansion of spirituality into a sense of being in partnership with God in all lines of work, physical and intellectual, to further the evolutionary development of a new part of creation: the noosphere.

- Think about the sum effect of the past thirty-five days of meditations. Looking over your journal or notes on the retreat materials, discern the growth or change in your sense of the sanctity of your work.

Now, together with a whole world of spiritual brothers and sisters, draw in the Spirit with your breath and go about your work "so that the Universe may be raised . . . to a higher level." Amen.

Suggestions for Group Prayer

Passages from the Scriptures or from Teilhard's works that might be useful in each week's prayer service are listed here. With the exception of week 1, the readings reflect the theme of the previous week's meditations. The closing prayer service celebrates Christ's transformation of all facets of our work experience into building blocks for the noosphere, the holy City of God.

Week 1: Vocation or Calling

Wisdom 7:7–10,15–16. Seek wisdom and understanding.
Matthew 5:13–16. You are the salt of the earth.

Week 2: Preparation

John 14:1–6. In God's house are many places.
Acts 8:26–39. Philip helps the Ethiopian eunuch to understand.
Psalm 139:1–12. God knows us and what we need.

Week 3: Mission

Proverbs 1:2–9. Listen and learn more.
Psalm 119:169–176. May I live only to praise God.
Luke 2:41–52. Jesus goes about God's business.

Week 4: Success

Joshua 1:1–3,6–7,9. God blesses Joshua.
Psalm 105:37–40,43–45. God leads the people out of slavery.
Matthew 10:1,5–8,16. Jesus gives the Apostles authority.

Week 5: Setbacks

"Hymn to Matter" from *Hymn of the Universe,* by Pierre Teilhard de Chardin, pages 65–68:

> "Blessed be you, harsh matter, barren soil, stubborn rock: you who yield only to violence, you who force us to work if we would eat. . . .
>
> "Blessed be you, mighty matter, irresistible march of evolution, reality ever newborn; you who . . . force us to go ever further and further in our pursuit of the truth. . . .
>
> "I acclaim you as the divine *milieu,* charged with creative power, as the ocean stirred by the Spirit, as the clay molded and infused with life by the incarnate Word. . . .
>
> "Your realm comprises those serene heights where saints think to avoid you—but where your flesh is so transparent and so agile as to be no longer distinguishable from spirit.
>
> "Raise me up then, matter, to those heights."

Psalm 105:24–32. God sends darkness on Egypt.
John 14:15–21. God will send the Spirit to be with us forever.

Week 6: Transformation and Transfiguration

Ruth 1:1–9. Naomi blesses Ruth and Orpah and tries to send them home.
Psalm 71:1–6,9,17–21. In God, we take refuge.
Mark 9:17–27. Jesus heals the possessed boy and his father.

Closing Prayer Service of the Retreat

All Pray
Open our eyes, we pray, to a bolder comprehension of the universe, and show yourself to those who love you, as the higher soul and the physical center of your creation.

A Reading from "The Mass on the World"

It is done.

Once again the Fire has penetrated the earth.

Not with sudden crash of thunderbolt, riving the mountain-tops: does the Master break down doors to enter his own home? Without earthquake, or thunderclap: the flame has lit up the whole world from within. All things individually and collectively are penetrated and flooded by it, from the inmost core of the tiniest atom to the mighty sweep of the most universal laws of being: so naturally has it flooded every element, every energy, every connecting link in the unity of our cosmos; that one might suppose the cosmos to have burst spontaneously into flame. (*Hymn of the Universe*, p. 16)

All Pray

Bless Yahweh, O my soul.

. . . .

You make fresh grass grow for cattle,
and fruit for your people.
You bring forth food from the earth:
wine to make them rejoice,
oil to make them happy,
and bread to make them strong.
The trees of Yahweh are well watered—
those cedars of Lebanon.
Here the birds build their nest;
and on the highest branches, the stork has its home.
For the wild goats there are the mountains;
badgers hide in the rocks.
You made the moon to mark the seasons;
the sun knows the hour of its setting.
You form the shadows, night falls,
and all the forest animals prowl about—
the lions roar for their prey
and seek their food from God.
At sunrise they retire,
to lie down in their lairs.
People go out to work
and to labor until the evening.

(Psalm 104:1,14–23)

A Reading from John 17:1,17,20–22

> [Jesus] looked up to heaven and said, . . . "The hour has come; glorify your Son so that the Son may glorify you."
>
> "Sanctify them in the truth; your word is truth."
>
> "I ask not only on behalf of these, but also on behalf of those who will believe in me through their word, that they may all be one. As you . . . are in me and I am in you, may they also be in us, so that the world may believe that you have sent me. The glory that you have given me I have given them, so that they may be one, as we are one."

Prayers of the Gathered Faithful

Grant us the remembrance and the mystic presence of all those whom the light is now awakening to the new day. [Pause for a moment of silence.]

One by one, gracious God, we see and love all those whom you have given us to sustain and charm our life. [Petitions, thanksgivings, and intercessions may be offered.]

One by one, also, we number all those who make up that other beloved family that has gradually surrounded us, its unity fashioned out of the most disparate elements, with affinities of the heart, of work, of mission, and of thought. [Petitions, thanksgivings, and intercessions may be offered.]

And again, one by one, we call before us the vast anonymous army of living humanity, those who surround us and support us though we do not know them. [Petitions, thanksgivings, and intercessions may be offered.]

We pray for the transformation of all things in the world to which this day will bring increase, all those that will diminish, and all those, too, that will die. [Petitions, thanksgivings, and intercessions may be offered.]

We remember before you those in office, laboratory, and factory who, through their vision of truth or despite their error, truly believe in the progress of earthly reality and who today will take up again their impassioned pursuit of the Light. [Petitions, thanksgivings, and intercessions may be offered.]

All Pray

I will make the whole earth my altar and on it I will offer you all the labors and suffering of the world. [At this time, those who wish to do so are invited to offer to God some object that is symbolic of their life and vocation, to help to build up the noosphere, the Reign of God.]

Close with the Lord's Prayer

Acknowledgments *(continued)*